RESTAURANT

from

SCRATCH

HOW TO TRUST YOUR HEART, LISTEN TO THE MARKET AND BEAT THE ODDS

JELYNNE JARDINIANO

RESTAURANT

from

SCRATCH

HOW TO TRUST YOUR HEART,
LISTEN TO THE MARKET AND BEAT THE ODDS

JELYNNE JARDINIANO

Published by Advantage, Charleston, South Carolina.
Member of Advantage Media Group.

ADVANTAGE is a registered trademark and the Advantage colophon is a trademark of Advantage Media Group, Inc.

Printed in the United States of America.

ISBN: 978-1-59932-102-8
LCCN: 2010909685

This publication is designed to provide accurate and authoritative information in regard to the subject matter covered. It is sold with the understanding that the publisher is not engaged in rendering legal, accounting, or other professional services. If legal advice or other expert assistance is required, the services of a competent professional person should be sought.

Advantage Media Group is proud to be a part of the Tree Neutral™ program. Tree Neutral offsets the number of trees consumed in the production and printing of this book by taking proactive steps such as planting trees in direct proportion to the number of trees used to print books. To learn more about Tree Neutral, please visit www.treeneutral.com. To learn more about Advantage's commitment to being a responsible steward of the environment, please visit www.advantagefamily.com/green

Advantage Media Group is a leading publisher of business, motivation, and self-help authors. Do you have a manuscript or book idea that you would like to have considered for publication? Please visit www.amgbook.com

DEDICATION

I dedicate this book to my best friend and husband ~ Robert Fiorito.

ACKNOWLEDGEMENT

You are all the positive forces that made my journey worthwhile and my dream possible. Because you decided to show up and step up in your own lives, you enabled me to do the same. Thank you for your trust, faith, hope and most of all, your love.

My everything, Robert
My parents, Mapalad + Violeta
My dear brother, Jerome
My sister, Janis + brother in law Ted
My brother, Jan + sister in law Mayette
My dearest friend, Claudia
My childhood confidant, Elise
My right hand gal, Andrea
My landlord, Steve + Maria
My favorite politician, Steve
My haven at Pound Ridge
My encouragement at Cornell
My family at Advantage Media Group

TABLE OF CONTENTS

Entrepreneurship means you have to put yourself out there and take chances at doing what you love. My road led from ice cream to a full-scale restaurant, with detours into financing and politics. Now it's your turn!

The top 10 pieces of conventional wisdom about opening a restaurant – including failure rate, money and workload – can be discouraging. Don't listen to naysayers; instead, do your own research. Here are many sources and strategies.

Your concept may be creative, but the business is not about you; it's about fulfilling the needs of your target market and customers. Here are some questions to ask yourself and others. Put your feet on the street and do your own market research.

A personal vision will set your place apart. Start out broadly, then narrow your vision to answer this question: "What is your compelling reason for existence?" I've provided a list of powerful points of differentiation for restaurants. Consider what concept is best for you.

Chapter 9: Opening — 151

A grand opening vs. a soft opening. But, however you open your doors, be sure you have tested the menu and hired and trained the staff well in advance. Be especially diligent of your operations and services during the first six months, which will be a true test.

Chapter 10: Growing With the Business — 157

A few last bits of advice: Get accustomed to not knowing everything. Be open to learning on the fly and responding quickly to changes and challenges. Contact me with questions. Most of all: Go for it!

INTRODUCTION

T he fastest road to failure in the restaurant business starts with a three-letter word. I learned of it on the first day of my food and beverage class at Cornell. And I stand by it. The word is *ego*. Ego based restaurants usually are excessive projects, designed to make its owner look good and typically miss the mark with its intended guests. But it's also the same ego that leads someone to another type of failure – the failure to get started. We become so afraid of failing and being labeled as one, that we'd rather protect our ego than pursue our dream.

Restaurant from Scratch is my experience pursuing my dream to be a restaurant owner. It details how I got started in the industry, to creating a bar with a small budget right out of college and growing it into a busy and successful restaurant over time. I opened with no capital reserve and a city law that limited my hours of operation. I was young and had limited experience. And while your circumstance will be different from mine, the underlying theme is the same: start where you are and take action regardless of your circumstance.

Every time someone shares the dream of having his own restaurant, money almost always gets brought up as the key to him having it. Yes, money can get you open. But to have and to hold onto that restaurant for the long haul requires much more than cash. The sooner you become aware of the other resources you have besides money, the better equipped you will be to start and grow your own restaurant.

I decided to trace my steps and document it in this book after being repeatedly asked by friends and patrons for advice on starting a restaurant or similar business. I take you through the stages, beginning with your conceptual idea, to developing that concept, to transferring it from paper to its physical equivalent, to effectively marketing it, to the opening day and into your first six months.

At its best, I hope my book will help get you closer to the truth in your heart. Only you know what that is because only you know what feels right, what you fantasize about and what road you feel destined to take. The search for truth is internal. And it is sometimes sparked by outside sources, from people, places, things, and even from thin air. The goal of this book is to be one such source that ignites and guides the desire in your heart.

In love and service,

Jelynne Jardiniano

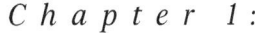

Chapter 1:

MY STORY

TWO STEPS BACK, ONE BIG LEAP

I had my life planned out. I was studying at one of the best schools in the country with my eyes set on being a high-paid lawyer. But the more I tried to will myself to committing to that career, the more miserable I became. And when a relationship that I cared for came to a sudden end, I headed into a depression that I had never known. Unmotivated to get out of bed, I was surprised to make it past my first year in college. My entire life up to that point was defined by my academic achievement, and for the first time, I didn't care. My body reacted by making me so ill that I had to take time off from school.

Being at home and feeling left behind by my peers dug me deeper into despair. The girl who had been so sure of herself disappeared. I slept for hours on end, hoping to wake up and find that it was just a dream.

I slept away my sorrows for some time before deciding to occupy myself with something else. I applied for the easiest job a student could get and was hired as a hostess for a small seafood restaurant in the upper west side of New York City. The job was simple enough - look pretty, smile and seat guests. I cleaned menus, refilled salt and pepper shakers and answered the phone. I had to know the guests by name, so I was encouraged to talk and become friends with the regulars. I did my simple job well and took pride in it. Not fully realizing it at the time, I slowly started to come back to life.

That was more than ten years ago. And I made that world my life. Little did I know that it would lead me to become an entrepreneur.

BORN OR MADE

I have often heard the question, "Are entrepreneurs born or made?" I believe that we are all born with the potential to become an entrepreneur, and those who do were *influenced*. For most of my life, being an entrepreneur did not enter my mind. But when I discovered a love for what I was doing, and found an environment that supported it, things started to change.

Upon returning to school, I thought I would become a restaurant manager. It paid a decent salary, and most of all, I would be in an environment I loved so much. But three more years of school proved to influence me beyond a list of careers. My professors spoke to us as if we were already business owners. They carried the conviction, long before I did, that their students would one day be running or owning a business. I started to believe them. And began playing with the *idea*.

By my junior year, my mind was set to become an entrepreneur. I liquidated a few thousand dollars from a mutual fund that my sister started for me and formed a company that was supposed to manufacture candy. My inspiration came from the Asian snacks that I enjoyed, and the first product was supposed to be Japanese mochi ice cream. My research, which included a trip to a trade show in Tokyo, eventually led me to a small mochi factory in New Jersey. I thought that the best way to start was to hire the company to make my own brand of ice cream.

That summer of my junior year, I was at Cornell taking classes. I ordered 50 cases of mochi ice cream, totaling a thousand pieces, in four different flavors. In my dorm room was a commercial freezer that was so big, it had to be disassembled to fit through my door. Weeks went by and I had sold not one piece. I wanted to approach the university cafeteria or the local grocery stores, but didn't. Fear set in and I found myself unable to move a freezer full of ice cream.

More weeks went by and I still had not done anything with my inventory. The reality was, I had to sell and was fearful of the consequences of it. What if I were rejected? Could I handle the embarrassment? Why would they buy from me? Who was I kidding? A recurring voice inside also kept telling me, "If you want to be an entrepreneur, go out there and sell it on the street." I ignored it.

I did everything that an entrepreneur was supposed to do. I incorporated my company, invested in research and development, secured a supplier, had a good product and a target market. But when I froze in fear to sell my goods, I realized the missing ingredient. I had yet to embody the entrepreneurial spirit.

Learning how to start a business is simple. Information is plentiful and available to anyone seeking it. But starting a business does not turn someone into an entrepreneur. One is a technical process and the other is a personal one. It is when the two work in tandem that the magic happens.

One weekend afternoon, I decide to take the plunge. I stepped out of my dorm room with a cooler full of mochi ice cream and hit the streets of Cornell's college town. I found a corner location, put up my sign and began selling my goods. My nerves were so unbearable that I thought I was going to vomit. But I made my first sale, and then my second, and then the next and with each sale, I began having more fun with it. By the end of the afternoon, I sold it all and as I was making my way back to my room, students were flagging me down for more.

My little college experiment was a big lesson on what all entrepreneurs must be willing to do: put themselves out there. Being in business means being vulnerable to rejection, ridicule and criticism. And it is for this reason that most would-be entrepreneurs fall short of their dream. It is not easy, especially when it seems that we have so much to lose. But having crossed this line before, I can tell you that all you lose is fear and what you gain is control of your life.

DOING WHAT YOU LOVE

Part of the reason I thought of having a manufacturing business was because I could hide behind my products and not have to put myself out there. When I put that fear behind me, it became clear that what I really wanted to do was to have a restaurant.

My work in restaurants is young compared with that of many of my peers in the industry, some who have dedicated their entire lives. While there is more to learn, my inspiration in sharing what I know comes from my experience in accomplishing more than I stood a chance to in a short period of time. It is a testament that starting a business under any circumstance is possible for the person who believes it and is committed to do the work.

I pursued opening a restaurant right after college, at a time when I didn't yet have a job and was still living with my parents. I searched for spaces for rent and met resistance from landlords looking for a restaurateur with existing locations or a person who had sizable capital. I had neither, but continued my search until I found an opportunity where those criteria didn't matter. I found it in the downtown area of Jersey City, New Jersey.

I negotiated six months of free rent, thinking it would give me enough time to find funding. But I was wrong, as a year would go by before the money showed up (story in Chapter 4). I raised $150,000, half of which went toward buying a liquor license. I was grossly under-funded and had even more challenges ahead. The location of my restaurant and bar, which I called LITM (for Love Is the Message), was in a zone that was restricted by a city law that ended drinking hours early. I found myself in a hostile environment between local neighborhood associations wanting to keep the zone restriction and Jersey City politics.

Going into our seventh year (at the time of writing this book), the picture is different from when I first started LITM. I got the city law changed two years after opening. Our annual sales have hit close to $1 million. I have managed to grow the business with

80 percent less money than it takes to build an average restaurant doing that kind of sales. And as the business continues to grow by double digits, I am having more fun and more time for myself.

EXPERIENCE IN DOING

This book takes you through my journey in creating a restaurant from scratch. I start from the beginning stages, when the restaurant is just an idea, and end with what to expect during the first six months of being open. Everything I share with you has been my first-hand experience. And though I have created an extensive resource, the work must ultimately be done by you. This book is one of the many steps along your way. Do the most you can each day. Your restaurant is waiting to happen.

Chapter 2:

THOUGHTS, IDEAS AND INFORMATION

R ight now, your restaurant is just an idea. How you think about that idea will determine most of the actions you take. Your thoughts shape the decisions that you make. And it is for this reason that I start our journey on the subject of thought.

If we were to compare our thoughts to our present circumstances, we would find a cause and its effect. Conscious of it or not, thoughts are constantly being affirmed in our mind and enacted in our lives. And unless we take control of how we think, popular beliefs and opinions stand ready to make up our minds for us.

Your ability to think for yourself will be one of your biggest tests as a budding entrepreneur. Our need for approval by others is so important to us that we fear thinking differently and risking rejection. People will discourage you and offer information that will go against your entrepreneurial endeavors. Self-defeating thoughts will creep in. Your duty to yourself will be to search for the truth, to question opinions and assumptions that don't tell the whole picture.

When my restaurant was just an idea, I made a point to learn how other restaurateurs made it happen. I researched how they overcame obstacles, how they turned one restaurant into multiple operations, and how they approached the world. I looked not at just what they did, but who they were being to achieve what they did. I put them in my shoes and imagined how they would have approached a situation or overcome an obstacle. I started to think like they would because they were the people I wanted to be.

THE TOP 10 THOUGHTS

These are the top 10 thoughts that I have heard through the years. They have been told many times by people related and unrelated to the industry and cited by reputable institutions. And yet they fail to represent a true picture of the restaurant business. Whenever you find yourself being told a limiting thought similar to one of these, ask whether it has been the experience of every restaurateur. Because unless these supposed facts are indisputable, they are inaccurate and unworthy of your complete acceptance.

THOUGHT NUMBER 1: *The restaurant failure rate is 90 percent during the first year.*

This is the most prevalent and perhaps the laziest statistic about the industry. And yet no one could ever quantifiably prove it. Years back, American Express used this statistic in a marketing piece. When asked where they got the information, they wrote they couldn't cite a particular source. Go to www.restaurantfrom-scratch.com/AmexLetter to see a copy of their admission.

In 2005, Dr. H.G. Parsa, a professor at Michigan State University at the time, tested this failure rate myth. He researched restaurant failure rate over a three-year period in three local markets in Ohio. He found that after the first year, 27 percent of restaurant start-ups failed; after three years, 50 percent; and after five years, 60 percent. He went on to show that at an actual 90 percent failure rate, all restaurants would be nonexistent in 94 years.

My first rejection from a bank came with a letter supported by the 90 percent statistic. This initial rejection could have been enough for me to quit if I had not made a conscious effort to find other facts to the contrary.

THOUGHT NUMBER 2: *You need years of experience to open and run a restaurant.*

Experience is a popular word in business. Some will claim that with all their experience, the business will be a sure success. While others will be told, by others and even themselves, that because of their lack of experience, starting a business would be impossible. But what is the true value of experience when it only comes by being involved in the actual thing? If I had waited until I had experience in selling ice cream, I wouldn't have experienced selling it when I did. If I waited to have experience in running a restaurant, I wouldn't have opened it one year after college. And in writing this book, if I had waited until I had a lifetime of experience being a restaurateur, it would never have been written at this time.

The value of having experience is when you are having *the* experience. Experience is not a future criterion that you have to meet. Experience is now. It is the exact moment that you decide to get involved.

Passion, dedication, and determination can't be measured in years of experience. I know this because I opened my restaurant/bar one year after college without knowing how to make a single cocktail or knowing how to cook. The only experience I had in the industry was as hostess, server, assistant party-planner and banquet manager. From those low-level positions, I jumped to being a restaurant owner. I was 19 when I discovered my passion for this business. Five years later, I had my own place.

THOUGHT NUMBER 3: *You need a lot of money to start a restaurant.*

Although sufficient financing is vital, most successful restaurateurs start with less than $100,000. The financial management of the restaurant is more important. Plenty of multimillion-dollar restaurant projects have flopped in a matter of months. Having a lot of money may get you started, but it does not guarantee success.

Lack of money shouldn't be a reason to abandon your business idea either. Your creativity is worth much more. Use your imagination to find alternative ways into the business. (More on this subject in Chapter 7.)

THOUGHT NUMBER 4: *You must work seven days a week with no vacation and no life.*

If you go into business with this expectation, that's what you're going to get. Restaurateurs who understand their business cycle take off weeks and even months at a time for a vacation. A common time to take off is the week after Thanksgiving, when most restaurants slow down after the holiday. Other common vacation times are right after the new year and the entire month of August.

You can also serve one or two of the day parts. Which means you can choose to be open only for dinner or just serve breakfast and lunch. And you can even go beyond the typical Monday off for restaurants. Some restaurateurs have designed their operation to be open a few days a month and closed for the rest of the time. The decision is yours. You control the schedule of your business and make rules that support what you want in your life.

THOUGHT NUMBER 5: *There is too much competition.*

The fear of competition comes from the idea that you may not measure up. Decide once and for all that you are more than capable to succeed. Your genuine love for this business is your true business advantage.

Don't let the fear of competition stop you. Focus on creating and adding more value to peoples' lives and you will never have to fear competition. Competition isn't a threat. It's an affirmation that a need exists. The best example is the ever-thriving Chinatowns, which are packed with much of the same thing — Chinese restaurants.

THOUGHT NUMBER 6: *You don't make money with restaurants.*

I know restaurateurs who have created dream lifestyles for themselves and their families, and half of them own one restaurant. People who make this statement may have had this experience, but it is not the case for everyone in the business. Otherwise, restaurants would cease to exist. The successful restaurateurs who have created tremendous wealth for themselves disprove this popular thought.

THOUGHT NUMBER 7: *A busy restaurant is a successful restaurant.*

Busy-ness and efficiency are separate. Volume is only a portion of a restaurant's business health. You need to consider your efficiency and how that translates to controlled costs, profitability, and positive cash flow.

Every restaurateur's greatest insecurity is not being busy. The first couple of years into my restaurant, I was too focused on being busy. I charged prices comparable and sometimes lower than other restaurants and justified it with the volume that we'd create. But I didn't attract my ideal guests using the low-price tactic. So I dared to raise my prices and increase the level of service. The volume decreased shortly after, but I attracted better guests and worked less for more money. Evaluate your activity, time, and effort. You may be more occupied with being busy than being profitable.

THOUGHT NUMBER 8: *Good food makes a restaurant.*

Restaurants are complex and dynamic and good food is but one aspect of a multitude of factors that make a restaurant. This is why casual chain restaurants flourish. Their average food is offset by consistency, convenience, a lively atmosphere, and value for the money. Restaurants today must define what they are well beyond the type and quality of cuisine being served. Having good food is just starters.

THOUGHT NUMBER 9: *You have to be present in your restaurant all the time.*

Having systems in place and the right people to execute them is the answer to this popular misconception. Every great business thrives on having quality people running concise systems. This is how franchising is possible. Create systems for your restaurant that enable others to do most of the work for you. That allows you to monitor your business and eliminates the need to be present at all times.

Developing an effective system will take time and tweaking along the way. I started formulating my system a year into being in business. I realized that much of what I knew to do was kept in my head and explained why I always had to be there. The simple act of writing down all of the things that I did myself enabled me to delegate those duties to a staff that was hungry for more responsibility.

THOUGHT NUMBER 10: *This business isn't glamorous.*

What could be more exciting than doing what you love and being paid to do it? Sure, you'll wind up doing whatever it takes to run your business (such as cleaning toilets or being the dishwasher in the event of a no-show). But the satisfaction of doing so for your place is the true glamour.

Even people in the industry make this comment. I interpret this negativity as a sign that they're ignoring their intuitive sense to do something else. I worked in the kitchen for a year and a half because I thought I couldn't afford to hire a chef. Tension and resentment for all the hours I had to spend cooking started to surface. I finally asked myself whether I wanted to be a chef. The answer was no. The next week I hired our first executive chef. I found the business could afford it and our food sales increased by 15 percent.

If I had continued to do what I thought I should be doing, instead of what I truly wanted to do (which was developing the business), I would have bought into this myth too.

Everyone has different experiences and develops their own opinion based on those experiences. Spend the time to uncover facts that will help you make intelligent decisions. Taking control of your life starts with taking control of your thoughts.

THE POWER OF INFORMATION

Every day, the world's financial markets open and spiral up or down based on information. Money is either lost or gained by the interpretation of information. Creating your restaurant follows the same idea. You will need a vast amount of research, interpretations of it, and decisive action based on its accuracy. If you want to make money doing business, then make gathering information a priority.

I knew to stop pursuing law when I cringed at reading the material. There would be times when I couldn't get past a paragraph before falling asleep. That changed as soon as I found my passion for restaurants. If I wasn't in class, I used my spare time reading industry magazines in the library or surfing the Internet for the latest happenings. I still have an insatiable need for relevant information for business and life. I read countless books and magazines, and attend seminars and trade shows.

When Warren Buffett started investing, he was as unknown as any entrepreneur who first starts out. He sought profit-and-loss statements from publicly owned companies, which anyone can access and costs nothing. He researched, interpreted and took action on the information he acquired and built a fortune based on intelligent and intuitive interpretation of information.

If you're beginning your entrepreneurial career, be patient with yourself and be diligent in becoming a lifelong student of your craft. Your initial focus is to be a magnet for information, to open your eyes and observe successful businesses, to ask thoughtful questions. Quality information is abundant and accessible. The more informed you are, the better suited you'll be to make lucrative business decisions when the time comes.

SOURCES OF INFORMATION

When I was doing my initial research, many of the trade publications asked for a company name and federal identification number to acquire a subscription. Some publications no longer require that, but many still do. It is a three-step process to establish this criteria, and worth the effort to get valuable trade information:

1. Create a company name for your restaurant and get registered as a corporation or a limited liability company (LLC). You can do this online for any state. The cost ranges from less than $100 to more than $300. It is well-worth this investment to get the information you need.

2. After you have filed your company name, apply for an employer identification number, or EIN. Go to www.irs.gov and apply online for an EIN. With this number, you are now recognized as a company doing business in your industry. Even if you're not doing actual business, you will still need to file tax documents. Simply state you are not yet doing business or have not hired anyone.

3. With your EIN, you are eligible for free subscriptions to trade magazines. Here are a few of my favorite publications and online resources.

FREE TRADE MAGAZINES:

- Sante: http://www.isantemagazine.com

- Market Watch: http://www.marketwatchmagazine.com

- Food Arts: www.foodarts.com

- Restaurant Business: www.hotelresource.tradepub.com

- Specialty Food Magazine: www.specialtyfood.com

- Gourmet News: www.gourmetnews.com

- BizBash: www.bizbash.com

- PMQ Pizza Magazine: www.pmq.com

Paid-subscription magazines:

- Nation's Restaurant News: www.nrn.com

- Imbibe: www.imbibemagazine.com

- Food & Wine: www.foodandwine.com

More trade magazine listings can be found on the following Web sites:

- www.freetrademagazines.com/food-beverage-magazines/

- www.hotelresource.tradepub.com

- www.mesda.com/free_magazines/Food_Beverage.aspx

Online resources

- RestaurantFromScratch.com

- RestaurantOwner.com

- RestaurantResults.com

- Register for Google alerts for "restaurants" or anything else of interest

TRADE SHOWS

Trade shows are an important resource for your continuous education. When I was still a student, I enjoyed going to those events and would imagine hiring the vendors in the future. Restaurateurs at every level make a point to attend these events. The registration fees are usually less than $100 and covers two to three days of exhibitions, classes and workshops. Here are the shows I attend every year or every other year:

- NRA Show in May, Chicago: www.show.restaurant.org

- International Hotel/Motel & Restaurant Show in November, New York City: www.ihmrs.com

- Fancy Food Show Summer in June, New York City: www.specialtyfood.com. This show travels the major cities in the United States. Check its Web site for upcoming shows.

- Nightclub & Bar Las Vegas Show in March: www.ncbshow.com. I have never attended this show but it is among the largest in this category.

You will find ads for various shows and industry-related events in most of the trade publications. These are great opportunities for you to meet others with your same passion, get exposed to the latest trends, and have fun while working.

Chapter 3:

THE MARKET

IT'S ALL ABOUT THE MARKET

Through the years, people have shared with me their idea of the next great restaurant. Whether these people were sharing their thoughts on a whim or were aspiring restaurateurs is beside the point. Their approach is a common cause for failure. This thought is based on what they want and not on what the market desires.

While the fun may be in creating the concept, the disappointing part is finding out after you have opened that the market does not care for what you have to offer. Instead, do all you can to understand your guest. Your business exists to serve people and to be a valuable part of their lives. Have an answer to an unfulfilled desire. Find out what that is, and the right concept will follow.

In an article in the May 2009 issue of *Sante* magazine titled "Time for a Change", Connecticut-based restaurateur and chef Jonathan Rapp shared the costly misunderstanding of his market. He identified himself as an Alice Waters disciple and was convinced that his affluent town would have the same interest in local and seasonal cuisine. Two years into the business and almost bankrupt, Rapp realized that he needed broader appeal and had alienated much of the conservative rural potential clientele. He cited the menu as too limited and challenging. His communal style seating was also frustrating for customers who wished to have their own tables and privacy. But his major revelation was in having what he called Chef's Syndrome. "It was all about me and what I wanted. As a chef, I was arrogant and rigid. Many people found the restaurant intimidating and didn't feel welcome or comfortable."

Chef Rapp changed his restaurant to meet the needs of his market in time to turn his business around. Some owners don't get a second chance. You want to get it right the first time. To do that, start by being a good listener. Stop the urge to dictate what *you* want your restaurant to be and listen to what *others* are looking for. Your role, throughout your career and especially in the early stages of your restaurant's development, is to be a fact-finder. Glean what people are thinking, interpret what they are saying, and observe their behavior.

Learn from the mistakes and successes of others in the industry. The next time you go to your favorite restaurant or bar, ask yourself, *What is it about this place that I like so much?* You may find that the place feels like your second home. Or it makes you feel sexy and cool. Or maybe the staff makes you feel important and lifts up your spirit. Do the same thing for a failed restaurant. List all the possible reasons for its failure. This is a great exercise to develop your intuition.

Study businesses that are unrelated to restaurants. You may find an unexpected inspiration. The fast food drive-through was inspired by the drive-up windows at banks. Be interested in and curious about everything around you, because success leaves clues.

Write down the information you gather. Organize it with relevant articles and other research material. Being organized will help you have clarity about your market. And the clearer your thoughts, the more effective you will be in formulating a winning concept and pitching your idea to potential investors.

WHAT CAN YOU TELL ME ABOUT YOUR MARKET?

Market research may seem complex, institutional, and even out of reach. But the information that you are seeking is more apparent than you may think. When you know what to look for, market research will become effortless and intuitive.

From the start, I knew I wanted to serve my peers. They were, after all, a market I understood because of our demographic similarities. I took inventory of all that I knew about myself and started to paint a picture of a typical guest. I started with the basic demographics such as:

- Age

- Ethnicity

- Profession

- Income

- Education

- Social upbringing

- Home owner or renter

- Family size

- Hobbies

- Favorite television/cable programs

- Subscriptions to magazines

I continued to get more specific with what I knew about myself and documented information such as:

- Favorite authors

- Favorite fashion designers

- Favorite stores to shop for clothes and shoes

- Favorite cars

- What types of technology used

- Favorite brand of technology

- Do I cook at home? How often do I go out to eat in a month? Do I do home entertaining?

- Favorite restaurant, cuisine, bar, nightclub

- Places traveled

- Friends' profiles

KEEP ASKING

I looked at all the information about me and asked myself, *why?* Why did I choose a Mac over a PC? Is it because I was drawn to the design, image, function or flexibility over a PC? Why did I identify with a certain fashion designer? Is it because he or she represented who I wanted to be, did he or she stand for something that I valued, such as ingenuity and flair, or is it because the person was the hot designer of the time? The same goes for why I liked certain cars over others. My favorite at the time was Volkswagen. I identified with its approachable design, reputation, quality, and, most of all, it had a nice balance of image and function. It saw it as an elegant yet down-to-earth brand – similar to whom I thought I was as a person.

Our decisions are driven by emotions. We have a certain idea about ourselves, and our actions reinforce that idea. The strength of your concept will be measured by the extent that it connects with what your guests identify with and deem important in their lives.

Use the questions you asked yourself and repeat it for others. Start by asking your friends and acquaintances and have them ask their friends and acquaintances. Know what information you are looking for. Ask what type of restaurant they would like to see in their neighborhood. Ask questions that reveal underlying motives for their purchasing behavior. The way to get this information, without being intrusive, is to ask what brands they buy across different product categories. Brands are transparent with the image they want to project and what values they hope to represent. People who choose these brands are identifying themselves to some part of that culture. And to a certain extent, you can assume what is important to them and what motivates them to buy.

If your target market is not in your own neighborhood or a place familiar to your sphere of friends, then start by observing the area you have in mind. For example, if your restaurant will be located in a town different than yours, start by observing local behavior. Go to a nearby supermarket and see what products are being bought. Look at what cars are parked in the lot. Profile everyone that you see and take note of it. Are they young families? Older retired couples? Middle-aged mothers with college-age kids? What are they wearing? What kinds of announcements are being posted on the community bulletin board?

You may also consider hiring college students majoring in marketing to conduct formal research of your target market. Projects of this nature are commonplace for college students and they may be available to do it for a nominal fee. You can also contact marketing professors in colleges in your area and see if they can recommend students to help you. My experience with professors is that they are generous with their time, knowledge and resources. All you have to do is ask.

WHAT NEED EXISTS?

Our goal is to make your restaurant a hit right out of the gate. This is especially important when a restaurateur has limited capital. We can lessen the time it takes for your restaurant to be busy and profitable by having a deep understanding of the need that exists in the market. Make it *easy* for your guests to choose you. Start with what they want and desire.

I graduated from Cornell a year after the September 11th attacks. I moved back home to Jersey City, a city situated directly across the Hudson River from Manhattan, knowing that I would try opening my restaurant there. I got reacquainted with friends and picked up on a common sentiment among them. My peers wanted to stay close to home rather than go to New York City when choosing a place to drink and hang out. I attributed that to the shock that people still had from the attacks. The comfort of being close to home outweighed the uncertainty of commuting into New York City.

But we were frustrated at not having a New York City-type place in our own town. It seemed so odd, given our proximity to the endless choices of bars and restaurants in the city across from us. But it actually made sense. Prior to September 11th, Manhattan was the obvious choice to hang out. That changed. Jersey City residents wanted to stay within walking distance to home.

The timing was right. I did an extensive survey of the Jersey City downtown area and found the need that existed – a hip and friendly neighborhood place. Residents wanted to feel as if they were getting away to a place typical of NYC. They needed the same energy, sophistication, and sex appeal of the big city, but in the warmth of their own community.

Choose where you want your restaurant to be and be relentless in knowing everything about that town. Experience what it is like to be a resident there looking for a place to eat, drink, and hang out. Make a list of the places that already exist. Rate their popularity and document what they do right and where they miss the mark.

Categorize the existing restaurants and bars by the type of cuisine, level of service, ambience, location, price, and target market.

Compare that to what the people are looking for. You will start to uncover needs that exist, services that can be improved, and services that are altogether missing. Remember that needs and services are both tangible and intangible elements. A tangible service or need can be a family-style pizzeria, and intangibles are feelings and emotions that these places evoke.

In the next chapter we'll go over my favorite part of the restaurant development process - creating concepts. We will match the marketing with the vision and purpose of the restaurant to create a winning concept.

Read full interviews with Industry players on the Members section of the website, www.**RestaurantFromScratch**.com

Michelin-star chef, **Theo Schoenegger**

CFO of Chef Driven Restaurant Group, **Blanca Perez**

Restaurateur and Industry Veteran, **Piero Selvaggio**

Professor and Author of *Why Restaurants Fail*, **Dr. H.G. Parsa**

Chapter 4:

CREATING WINNING CONCEPTS

WHAT IS YOUR VISION?

I t's your right to love what you do and make money doing it. Match what the market needs to what your interests are and you'll do just that. Winning concepts have a power behind them. And that is your sincere and enthusiastic interest in giving the service and product that people want. The result is an authentic and fulfilling experience that both you and your customers benefit from.

Many businesses get started out of a solution that the founder was looking for but couldn't get. A simple premise like that is a great start because it came from a sincere interest. I was looking for a hip neighborhood place to relax and be with friends. And I found a larger market looking for the same thing. But I had to define what *hip* and *neighborhood* meant for me. This idea had to mean something to me. I knew that the soul of the restaurant depended on it. My vision of a hip and neighborhood place included: a modern space; fresh, eclectic menu; artistic culture; good music; friendly staff; and a warm and inviting, relaxed and casual atmosphere. This was a type of place that I would be excited about and want to go to myself.

This inimitable sincerity is especially important for independent restaurateurs, because it is part of our business edge. People sense a concept born out of a corporate boardroom and another born out of a person's vision and passion. People want to know the person behind the business and the personal story of how it came about.

The business is *about* you, but *for* the people. After doing the market research, focus on your vision for the concept. Think in broad ideas first, such as the feeling of the place. What are the emotions that you want people to feel when they enter? What lasting impression do you want them to leave with? What do you want to be known for? Think of everything that matters to you when you seek a dining and drinking experience. But always keep in mind whom this experience is for – your guests. Having said that, let's return to what motivates and makes you happy.

A restaurant is fun to the extent that the business supports the lifestyle you want. Many restaurateurs have bought into the opposite view that their lifestyle has to support the business. As someone starting from scratch, you have an opportunity to correct that. Decide now how you want your time to be spent and where you want your energy to be focused. Think of how you want to interact with your guests. Do you want to get to know them on a more personal level? Or would you rather focus on a business that runs on autopilot without the need of your face or presence?

Creating a concept is about creating an experience, an experience that should be enjoyable to you and your guests. Take your time to find the balance between giving your guests what they want in a way that you enjoy giving it to them. Your enthusiasm for your own business will give it its life over the long haul.

TIGHTEN UP YOUR CONCEPT

In the creative stages of your restaurant, you will be tempted to want to be all things to all people. I think that is a healthy way to start, as long as you do not end the same way. You should have more ideas than you can implement. And the more you expose yourself to successful restaurant operations, the more ideas you will naturally pick up. But as you move along the development process, those ideas should be chiseled to a tightly defined, unique concept.

The last thing the market needs is another plain old vanilla "me too" restaurant that does everything the same as its competitors. You want to hit the ground running once you open. And you won't be positioned to do that if you're indistinguishable from the rest of your peers. You don't have to take drastic measures, either. It could be a compelling reason that is based on convenience, menu appeal, or ambience. Whatever the reason is, it must be important to your target market – something that compels them to patronize your place, repeatedly.

Dan Kennedy, direct-marketing author and expert, asks this poignant question, "Why should I choose to do business with you over all of my other choices, including the choice of doing nothing?" Another way of asking this is, "What is your compelling reason for existence?" It's no secret that today's consumer is better informed about food and beverages and exposed to high-quality dining options. Given what already exists, your task of being noticed above the rest becomes more difficult. And the last thing you want to do is offer the same thing that everyone else is.

This *sameness epidemic* (or the "me too" problem) is cited by a 2009 study by Technomic, a food-industry market researcher, as a reason concepts failed to resonate with customers and a cause for their failure. Good service, good food, and a clean facility are ordinary expectations for guests and are not powerful points of differentiation. Value has always been a driving force in business. Companies that offer more value with fewer resources such as money, time, and labor thrive in any economic condition. But because we're in a tougher economic climate, value is at the top of mind for many.

Your restaurant has many ways to deliver value. Decide on which areas your concept will devote its focus and resources. Technomic lists six major categories that are powerful points of differentiation. Successful restaurants embody as many of these attributes as they can. Here is the list of categories that Technomic cites in its *Winning Restaurant Formula Report**:

Category #1: Lifestyle Integration

How well does the restaurant seamlessly blend into the lifestyle of its targeted customers? Consumers demand a satisfying restaurant experience that is also a good fit with their specific time, resources and dining occasion needs.

Category #2: Hospitality

Does the staff genuinely seem happy to see customers? Do customers truly feel that this is the place where they should be spending their discretionary dollars for an "Away From Home" meal occasion?

Category #3: Menu Desirability

What combination of characteristics makes the food and beverage offerings at this concept "pop" compared to consumers' other meal-solution options?

Category #4: Atmosphere

Does a visit to the restaurant just make the customer feel better?

Category #5: Concept Essence

Does the concept successfully communicate its core values, practices, and the foundational principles and elements of their unique operating business model?

Category #6: Manager Presence

Is it felt by both customers and employees? Customers want to feel like the restaurant (and its leadership face – the manager) genuinely appreciates their business. At the same time, this presence also provides employee support.

* (Source: *Technomic*. The full report can be found on Technomic.com)

If you think of your favorite eating and drinking places, chances are they deliver value across the six attributes listed above. These are the elements that contribute to a restaurant's success and deserve a great deal of your attention. Start by listing what other establishments are already doing right. Record what you think these places do best and how they capture their audience's patronage and loyalty. When you visit these places, observe and take notes on everything from lighting, décor, ambience, uniforms, menu design, fonts, color scheme, how you are greeted and spoken to, what you like most about the place, and what you don't like. Then choose the attributes that matter most to your concept and make them unique to your operation.

From the start, the vision of my concept centered on the feel of the place – the vibe. Downtown Jersey City was in need of an eating and drinking place with a New York look but a neighborhood feel. So I focused on the unique atmosphere of the concept. The space reminded me of a gallery with its long white walls and high ceilings. The neighborhood had a thriving artist community that often had functions in artists' own studio spaces. I envisioned a gallery-restaurant-lounge that would exhibit different artists every month and sell their work straight from our walls. I continued to tighten the concept around the gallery. I decided that the walls had to be white to be true to achieving a gallery look, feel, and purpose. The art on the walls would provide the color for the space and be a major determinant of the atmosphere. I knew that art would become the essence of our concept.

Midway into my restaurant's construction, it was apparent that a kitchen was out of our budget. I had to drop any attention on the food and develop the concept with our atmosphere. Art was a major focus, so I decided that everything about the place would be creative. The cocktail menu had to be original. The music had to be great. Films would be projected nightly with occasional independent film screenings. Our focus was on creating an intimate, creative space that guests would feel welcome and excited about.

Ultimately, the name chosen for the concept represented the atmosphere as well. *Love is the Message* was the initial name, but a twist was added by turning it into an acronym, *LITM*. Restaurants with obscure names (such *WD-50* in New York City) had already existed and proved to me that despite the oddity in a name, the place can still be understood.

From being an idea of a hip neighborhood place, the concept started to become tightly defined. It began to stand for something and to be for someone. We were going to be a part of the community, focus on making guests feel welcome and at home. Every day was going to have new experiences, while still being a familiar place. It was far from being another plain old vanilla concept. We were creating something new for a market that wanted it. The concept was a hit from the start.

CONCEPT IDEAS

Concepts are bound only by your imagination. Every year we see concepts that offer something better or new, or even something familiar. Let's take a look at a variety of concepts:

- *Retail hybrids* – these concepts combine a retail store with a restaurant. Combinations include a restaurant within a clothing store, such as the Armani/Ristorante in Giorgio Armani's Fifth Avenue store in New York City. Other combinations include a wine shop/restaurant, a beer shop/café or an ice cream parlor connected to a family restaurant. A goal of this type of operation is to give the guest more than one reason to choose their place to eat and/or shop. Convenience and a unique experience are major value-added bonuses to these types of places.

- *Cuisine* – many concepts focus their purpose and reason for existence on the type of food it serves. It seems to make the most sense to have the cuisine the main focus for quick-service and fast-casual operations because food at a modest price is their core focus. But for places with table service, there should be more of a compelling reason for their existence besides offering a certain type of cuisine.

- *Liquor* – there are concepts that are based on the type of alcohol they specialize in. An example is the Rhumbar in The Mirage Resort and Casino in Las Vegas. The Rhumbar was designed to look like a mojito cocktail, and specializes in rum drinks. A concept that focuses on the type of alcohol is at a high risk of being outdated very quickly. People's tastes change, and history is filled with the comings and goings of countless cocktails that were popular during a moment in time.

- *Theme* – theme restaurants are a lot of fun and can enjoy lasting success if the theme remains relevant and keeps its appeal to its targeted audience. The Rainforest Café and Walt Disney World are two great examples of theme destinations that continue to draw enthusiasm for the unique and memorable experience they give their guests. But theme restaurants don't have to be so elaborate as these two types. A theme restaurant can also be a sports bar, a restaurant in the theater district with celebrity pictures on the walls, or even a place like LITM – a restaurant-gallery that exhibits different artists every month.

- *Mobile* – mobile concepts include food trucks, carts, and windows. Food trucks and carts are no longer your old-time greasy food on wheels. Today they run the gamut of fresh burrito trucks, dumplings and noodles, sushi, gourmet breakfast, and dessert specialties. Window operations range from juice bars, to selling cupcakes and ethnic desserts such as Chinese mooncakes. With such a space constraint, these concepts are typically limited to a certain type of food.

When choosing your concept, project years ahead and determine whether it has the longevity to endure changes in the market. What is currently creating the demand for the concept? What could disrupt this demand in the near or distant future? Having the flexibility to change with the times is essential. If and when things change, will you have enough room to change and keep the interest of the marketplace?

Projecting ahead is obviously easier said than done. But looking at mistakes of others can give us the clues we need. Study restaurants that have failed and cite the reasons for their failure. Even if the concept is far removed from what you want to do, the lessons from business failures are universal.

Steak houses are a good example. They are known to draw corporate types with expense accounts. When the economy was doing well, the steak house segment grew exponentially and became even more niched within its own category. We saw steak houses that were targeting women, and others that were geared for metrosexual men versus jock types. It could either be targeting a younger clientele with a trendy interior or an older clientele with a rustic pub ambience. The prices ranged from moderate to very expensive. In a short period of time, markets became saturated with the steak house concept.

Once the economy began to slow, the segment went along with it. The steak houses were plentiful while their point of differentiation was minimal. Catering to a narrow niche group limited the reach and eventually became unsustainable. What was once wanted or desired, was suddenly deemed excessive, especially in operations where the ambience and decor were trendy and sleek.

The important lesson here is that your idea is going to be constantly challenged. There's a delicate balance between being consistent with what you want and also listening to what the market is asking of you. Over time this will become much clearer – this balance of being true to what you want but also offering what your guests need.

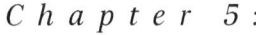

Chapter 5:

BUSINESS PLANNING

APPROACH TO MONEY

So many business ideas never get their chance because of money: not because of the lack of money, but because of the lack of faith of the entrepreneur. Every time anyone has approached me with an idea for a business, it's almost immediately countered with the *fact* that the person doesn't have the money to do it or know how to get it. By justifying his monetary position, the person negates his desire before it even has a chance to receive the money it eventually needs.

If you see money as an element beyond your control, focus your energy on the end result you want. When money is tight, we tend to fixate on the problem and unconsciously perpetuate the circumstance. Money is not the result you want. The money is a tool to get you the end result you desire – the restaurant, the chance to express yourself, the opportunity to add value to people's lives. Work toward your true end result. It may require you to further develop your business plan or continue your research. When you become your business, money will be in your control because of your confidence. The money is there waiting for you to receive it. Believe it.

Tracing my steps back to that time when I needed the money, my faith carried me through. There was no immediate sign of where the money would come from. And when time passed and the rejections came in, all that I had was my belief that the money I needed existed.

My restaurant had its start as an idea for a café. When I began looking for a space to rent, I was working as an assistant to an event planner making $30,000 a year. I was barely clearing enough money a month to make my school loan payments. I pursued my idea despite my lack of income and knowledge of where I would find an investor. In my pursuit to find a space, I faced rejection from landlords and management companies that told me that I didn't have enough experience or needed proof of my financial abilities. One day, I was walking down an avenue that I had walked down many times before, and saw a For Rent sign on the window. I called the number, met with the landlord, and had a great rapport with him. I would find out that not only was he looking to rent it out as a restaurant or café, but he also had a liquor license for sale. He didn't care that I was fresh out of college nor did he ask about my financial situation. My life took an unforeseen and remarkable turn. And all because I continued to pursue my business despite what I appeared to have lacked.

My landlord offered three months of free rent with the first year rate of $3,000 a month. I negotiated six months of free rent with a rate of $2,500 a month. I thought that six months would be enough time for me to find an investor. At this point, my family was out of the question, partly because I assumed they wouldn't support me and partly because they really didn't understand what I was trying to do and why I would want to do it. Having a corporate job was more of what they had in mind for me.

But I continued to develop my business idea. I revamped my business plan to reflect a restaurant and bar. And I continued to develop it with the belief that one day someone was going to invest in me. Every day after work I worked on my plan, did more research, played around with numbers, and created my financial projections. The time was ticking to the day I would have to pay rent. So I made the most of the time I had.

Three months into my job with the catering company, I was let go. I was also waitressing at night at a sushi restaurant, and that suddenly became my only source of income. I had to find another job. I interviewed for two months before finding a job as a banquet manager for a Southern Italian family-style restaurant on the Upper West Side of Manhattan. My salary was $10,000 more than my previous job, which provided me with just enough to make rent.

I began paying rent in January 2003 and would continue to pay it myself for many months ahead. Banks were quick to reject my plan, citing my inexperience, lack of equity, bad credit and the popular statistic that 90% of restaurants fail their first year. But during this time, I continued to move forward on things that I could afford to fund myself. I hired an architect to create blueprints for the space. He was inexpensive because he just drew what I told him to, with little to no creative input. But still, I was stretching my slim budget and there were months when I was completely short of rent. I asked anyone I knew to lend me the money. And I found that people whom I barely knew were the most willing.

This was a difficult time for me. And there were many nights when I cried myself to sleep. My landlord was getting concerned, and I sensed that he even felt guilty collecting rent on an empty space. I was close to being a year into the lease I had signed and my attempts at getting funding from banks or lending programs were unsuccessful. But I was so deep into this project that I forced myself no option but to continue trying. By this time my business plan was complete, as were my blueprints, list of vendors, and everything involving the restaurant. All I needed was the money.

My brother Jerome knew about the project and was the person most open to the idea from the beginning. I seriously approached him one day, with the blueprints in my hand. I knew this project inside out. I told him of the great location in the heart of downtown, the opportunity to own a liquor license, the cheap rent, and the need for a place that I had envisioned. He was convinced and gave me his support.

I used Jerome's credit for the company's first credit card, from Home Depot. We began exploring other lending institutions because we had his salary to make the application more desirable. A new and aggressive bank, Commerce Bank, approved us for a small amount of $85,000. That could buy us the liquor license with some left over, but it was only a portion of what we needed. Just as we were about to accept the loan, my mother sat us down. My brother-n-law had told her about our endeavor and she wanted to know exactly what we were doing. I told her all about the project and all that we had going for us. My brother told her that, no matter what, he'd find a way to get us the money. My mother did the unexpected. She offered to take a second mortgage on the home and suggested that we talk the rest of our siblings into doing the same. With my presentation at hand, I got my family to invest in me and in my idea.

If you asked me during this trying period *how* I was going to make my business happen, I wouldn't have had an answer. The wisdom was in my constant effort, the actions I took regardless of how uncertain the future was. I believed that the money would show up and I used all of my energy to prepare for that day. What I lacked in money I made up in faith. The beautiful part about this is that faith doesn't cost a thing. But because it's easier to succumb to appearances and the *way things supposedly are*, our ideas, dreams and aspirations don't get their chance because it seems too risky to have faith.

Continue with your idea even if you're uncertain where the money will come from. Do something every day to make yourself more informed, exposed and smarter about your business. You're preparing yourself for the moment when the money will present itself and ask that you be ready to receive it.

STRETCH THE DOLLAR

"Indulgence on a dime instead of indulgence on a dollar." Daniel Boulud uttered those words when describing his plans for opening another restaurant in a down economy. I believe this should be the approach to money in any economic climate. Being resourceful is not only attractive to your bottom line, but your customers will respect your effort. This is not to be confused with being cheap and skimping on the experience that the restaurant provides. But as Chef Boulud put it, you can achieve excellence with less expense. Spending the money just because you think you have it will catch up to the business. Restaurant projects that go over budget will be expected to perform above their ability. And regardless of the wealth or fame of the restaurant owner, the business cannot be sustained on a negative cash flow for an indefinite amount of time.

Avoid waste at all cost. Stretch every dollar from the budget of your restaurant. Find ways to achieve the same desired effect at a fraction of the expected cost. Explore your options for every facet of your business and make educated decisions. Demand the best products and services at the best prices. The world of business thrives on providing more value for less money. As Daniel Boulud puts it, "It's not about being cheap. It's about being proper."

PAY ATTENTION

I had a college professor whose father was in the restaurant business. He said the best that his father ever did for the entire 30 years of owning his restaurant was breaking even. His implication was that restaurateurs, namely the mom-and-pop restaurant owners, tend to manage their restaurant to get by instead of to get ahead.

I found myself on that track. During the construction phase of my restaurant, I laid out my plans in such detail that I knew exactly what every dollar was going to bring. I knew my numbers and my goal. And not a day went by that I didn't monitor and manage my money. But I didn't carry the same attention once our doors opened. The place was busy; money was coming in and going out.

I was paying the bills and too busy growing the business to be stuck in the details.

The truth was, I didn't look at my numbers because I was afraid of what I was going to find. I chose not to know anything rather than to risk finding out that I was a failure. It seems absurd, but that is what a person's fear can do.

I sought help from a reputable restaurant controller. I created an income statement that would be monitored from week to week. My beverage manager and chef had weekly purchasing budgets that they could not exceed unless the sales justified it. I cut unnecessary spending across the board – if it didn't directly affect the guest's experience and wasn't vital to our operation, I removed it from our operating expense. I itemized all of the outstanding invoices and formed a schedule to eliminate most of our debt. If sales for the week were off, I focused on being objective and proactive instead of getting emotional. I was paying attention to the money. And understood where it was all going.

PLENTIFUL AND AVAILABLE

Close to my fifth year in business, I was approached by outside investors to be their partners in future restaurant ventures. In all of my dealings with them, I came to understand that money must be used. Money is a tool. And it must be used for it to multiply. I understood the challenges of growing and preserving wealth. And whether money is used to buy stocks or invest in real estate, it has to be put to work for it to increase in value.

Businesses need money and money needs businesses. A business is a vehicle that makes it possible for money to increase in value. And the manner in which this is achieved is highly *organized*. Money moves through organized systems. Your business is such a system, and to create it will take a lot of planning.

Start with your business plan. Writing your plans down on paper makes them tangible, measurable, and more likely to happen. When you're forced to write it down, you're forced to be coherent and concise.

A well-developed business plan will organize your ideas and make the decision to invest in you a clearly good one. At the end of the day, people invest in people. Your confidence and competence will attract the money you need. And as you acquire the knowledge, the next step is to organize it in a written plan.

THE BUSINESS PLAN

The mere thought of writing a business plan can be enough of a daunting task. I've seen many budding entrepreneurs get stuck at this point in their business planning. The real problem lies in the ideas we have about a business plan. Many of us think it requires countless hours of writing, crunching numbers, and uncovering mounds of research to ultimately get it to a decent thickness. But this doesn't have to be, nor do I recommend it. I once heard someone say that you should be able to write your business plan on the back of a napkin. While this is an oversimplification, it reveals this truth – keep it simple.

Your goal isn't to write an award-winning novel. Your goal is to simply communicate how you're going to make money with your idea. Yes, definite content needs to be in your plan. Yes, it will take time. And yes, it could feel like a drag. But it doesn't have to be complicated. Nor should you get bogged down by thinking it has to be perfect. Treat your business plan as an evolving creation. Start with what you know and the information that you already have. And develop it as you go.

If you've thought of forgoing a business plan altogether, think again. A business plan will take you closer to realizing your business. An idea will remain an idea until a plan of action is created, and then acted on. Your business plan *is* your plan of action. The process of writing it out will clarify many of your thoughts and goals, especially in the beginning, when we tend to want to be all things to all people. What may have sounded like a good idea may look like an awful one on paper. Seeing our written word has the power to show us what is involved in making them happen. Sometimes, executing all of our ideas just isn't a viable option. And as a bonus, your confidence about your project will grow.

BEFORE YOU START

Overcoming any apprehension you may have about writing requires only one thing from you: Don't judge anything that you write, think, or say about your business. Focus on getting it down on paper and tweaking as you go. And when I say paper, it can be in your computer, your phone, pieces of scrap paper, a video or recording, etc. Move your ideas and thoughts from your mind to something tangible.

Most of this section on business planning pulls from what I did. It isn't meant to be followed exactly, but more of a visual guideline to what a plan can look like. Use it as a map, and depending on the needs of your own business, determine what content is pertinent and most effective in getting investors to believe in your idea. Write what you know, gather what you have, and get started! Action beats perfection every time.

TABLE OF CONTENTS

The table of contents can be used as an outline for the entire plan. For more examples, I recommend buying a book on how to write a business plan – preferably the one that lets you fill in the blanks. Don't let this list overwhelm you. Take it one section at a time. If ever you can't complete a section, move on to another part that you can start. The magic is in the motion. So let's get started!

Table of Contents

Executive Summary

Company Plan
>   Company Description
>   Goals/Objectives
>   Company Philosophy
>   Location
>   Lease
>   Services
>   Menu by Dayparts
>   Management

Market Analysis
>   The Restaurant Industry
>   Consumer Trends
>   Situation Analysis
>   Objective
>   Market Profile
>   Market Mix & Demo (Hudson County)
>   Restaurant Profile and Trends
>   Competition
>   Competitive Advantage & Positioning
>   Advertising & Media Strategy
>   Promotional Plan
>   Things to Remember

Financial Plan
>   Revenue Model
>   Funding
>   Payment Schedule
>   Assumptions

Appendices: Market Research, Financial Statements

Supporting Documents: Zoning Letter, Liquor License Check, Building Department Approval, Insurance Coverage, Resume

EXECUTIVE SUMMARY

An executive summary condenses your entire plan into one or two pages. It's meant to quickly grab the attention of a potential investor. This section is typically done last, when you can pull the major points from the other sections. Here's the executive summary of my own business plan:

Executive Summary

Company Overview

Superfresh Group Inc. will be a leading restaurant group offering fresh and innovative foodservice concepts to a regional, national and international market. Superfresh is a New Jersey State S-Corporation located in Jersey City, N.J. The company's first concept will be a two-floor full service tapas/bar/lounge/restaurant named *LITM*. The company's strategy is to establish *LITM* as its first restaurant chain concept.

LITM is short for "Love Is The Message." The *LITM* concept is based on people's need for self-expression. The restaurant will serve international food representative of people's different cultures, host live jazz, poetry slams and entertainment; and support the local artist community through opening exhibitions, exposure and recognition. LITM is a movement of good food, good times, and good company.

Mission Statement

To exceed guest expectations by consistently serving good food and giving great service in a fun and friendly environment, for a fair and reasonable price. To keep our employees happy by treating them with respect, honesty, and consideration. To be an innovator in foodservice concepts, while providing congenial hospitality in the community.

Market Overview

Despite the challenges to the nation and industry since September 11, Americans are frequently dining out and continue to visit their favorite restaurant. According to NRA consumer research, three out of four Americans say they will increase or maintain their frequency of dining out at full service restaurants. The research also found that 85 percent of consumers with household incomes of $50,000 or more, who are frequent patrons of full-service restaurants, are more likely than average to increase or maintain their frequency.

More Americans are choosing restaurants as secure meeting places to spend time with loved ones. After September 11, many local neighborhood restaurants reported that they were able to maintain their sales. 92 percent of adults agree that they feel safe when they are eating at a local restaurant. And seven out of 10 adults regard dining out with family and friends as an opportunity to socialize and consider it a better use of their leisure time.*

LITM will be a local establishment with a global vision. Research proves that the size of market, household income, age, lifestyle and education level of Jersey City residents fit the profile for restaurant/bar. Being centrally located in the prime Jersey City business and transit district, *LITM* has a strong potential for niche domination within its first 24 months of operation.

Management Team

Jelynne Jardiniano will be the Owner and General Manager of Superfresh Group. She is a graduate of Cornell University's School of Hotel Administration with an extensive education and practical experience in the food and beverage industry.

Financial Summary

LITM's revenue model is based on the primary sales of food and beverage products. Revenue is projected to grow through increased market share, increased prices and decreased expenses. The company expects sales and profitability over the next five years to be as follows:

Year	Avg Food Check	Avg Beverage Check	Sales	Net Income/Loss
1	$6.25	$3.50	$853,006	$130,393
2	$6.75	$4.00	$1,330,433	$389,843
3	$7.25	$4.50	$1,606,471	$546,415
4	$7.25	$4.50	$1,667,045	$580,064
5	$7.50	$5.00	$1,782,701	$632,428

To date, the owner has invested over $20,000 into product and market research, concept and business development, professional fees, leasehold deposits and other preliminary start-up costs. Superfresh Group is seeking to raise $270,000 from institutional investors in the form of a long-term loan. The owner and individual investors are funding an additional $90,000 – totaling the startup costs to $360,000. The uses for the $360,000 are summarized as follows:

Professional Services	$27,500
Permits	$1,150
Leasehold Improvements	$43,000
Furniture, Fixtures and Equipment	$68,000
Pre-Opening Expense	$4,000
Liquor License	$70,000
Food and Beverage Inventory	$15,000
Working Capital	$25,000
3 Months Operating Capital	$100,000
Telephone Installation & Deposits	$500
Utility Deposits	$950
Insurance Deposit	$2,500
Total Start-up Costs	$357,600

*Source: National Restaurant Association. *Restaurant Industry Forecast for 2002*

Another section I should have added is how the investor would be paid back his investment. I already had this information in the *Financial Plan* of my business plan. Be sure to include this information in your own executive summary.

COMPANY PLAN

The company plan includes every detail about the company. My business plan had eight sub-topics within the company plan. The following outlines the information for each subtopic.

COMPANY DESCRIPTION

- The corporate name, dba ("doing business as"), and type of corporation (S-corporation, L.L.C., C-corp, etc.).

- Describe the concept. What is its unique selling proposition? Hours of operation. How big is the space – is it more than one floor? How many seats – dining room, bar and lounge areas?

- What is the company's strategy? Will this location be the first in what will be a national chain? Will it be the first concept of a restaurant group? Will it be the only location you intend on opening, with an exit plan of selling the business after a certain number of years? This is the section where you address your long-term goals of the company. Investment thus far – quantify how much personal investment you've put into the business to date. What sort of research have you conducted?

- Qualify the team for your company. What are their names, background, and contribution to the company? Do you have a board of directors? Who are they and what do they bring to the table?

GOALS/OBJECTIVES

- List your long-term goals. This is typically looking five years ahead. Some of your goals can include how fast you plan to grow, the percentage that your sales will increase, your profit margin percentage, the size and strength of the team you plan to build, the percentage or section of the market that you will dominate, how much you plan to sell the business for and what the profit potential is, and anything that is in line with what you envision five years from now.

- List your short-term goals. This is typically within one to two years of operation. These goals usually cover the details of how you're going to run the operation. How you plan on fostering repeat business, your marketing campaigns, your weekly/monthly sales goals, your weekly/monthly net profit goals, your plans for community involvement, and anything that will keep you in line with your long-term goals.

COMPANY PHILOSOPHY

- What are the values of your company? What is important to your business? What are you committed to doing/accomplishing? Does your business have a theme or motto?

LOCATION

- Where will your restaurant be? What are the intersections? What is foot traffic like? Are you close to public transportation? Is the area part of a city-ordained "Restaurant Row"? Do you have great visibility? What types of businesses exist in that area? Are you in a business district or more of a neighborhood? Is there parking on the street, lots or garages for your customers? How does your area change during different times of the day – does it get busier at night or is it vacant after business hours? Developing this section of your business plan will require your careful observation of the location that you're proposing. Every investor knows the importance of a good location.

LEASE

- What are the terms of your lease? Are you renting at below market rate? Are you entering during a peak in the market? How long is your lease? Can you sell the lease? Do you have the right of first refusal in the event the building is sold? What other occupancy costs will you be responsible for?

SERVICES

- What services will you provide to your customers? These can include online ordering and reservations, party planning, taxi service, delivery service, bottle-holding, Internet access, catering etc. Services are what you offer your guests in addition to your core products of food and beverages.

Menu By Dayparts

- What is your menu going to be? Will you be serving breakfast, lunch, and/or dinner? Why have you chosen to offer your menu based on your customers' needs? Explain your menu and the reason for choosing it. Will the menu change over the course of the day? Does the crowd change over the course of the day?

Management

- People invest in people. Introduce your management, their experience, and the contributions that they will be bringing to the company. There is no need to exaggerate the information about your team. The reader will detect it and its appeal will be weakened. Instead, approach this section with a direct, practical, and objective optimism. Highlight each person's strength and his or her motivation for wanting to be a part of the business.

MARKET ANALYSIS

This is *the* most important part of your business planning. Your market analysis is the gathering of evidence that a need exists for your restaurant. But it's more than just finding information that supports your idea. It requires you to look at opposing views and facts and to think them through. You will be putting yourself at a major disadvantage if you ignore information that contradicts your proposed business. This type of information can only make your idea sharper and smarter. And it could reveal the best approach for your business.

When I first started developing the idea of my restaurant, I wanted to be all things to all people. I would visit my favorite places and document what I liked most about them. But I would eventually realize, as I was writing my business plan, that instead of trying to be like other places, I would be better off focusing on what their weaknesses were and making that my strength. As I developed the concept further, I continued to chisel down my ideas to a core list of strengths. And I made sure that they were in line with what I truly wanted to offer and what the market would truly want in their neighborhood.

Market research can be broken down between the market-at-large (the economy, national trends, moods and spending) and the micro-market (the local need, demographics, existing businesses). I hired a market research company to compile local statistics on the demographics and competition profile. It doesn't hurt to have a company do this work for you, but I think this information is readily available at your local library. I would instead hire a marketing company to develop and manage a campaign that will create buzz even before you open. With the availability of the Internet, social media, and mobile texting, a marketing company would best be used to manage all of these platforms for you. And don't think you have to look for a company per say. Students are growing up with this technology, and are so well-versed in it that they should command your serious consideration.

My business plan didn't address those marketing platforms because they didn't yet exist. So be sure to include them in yours. The following is the outline of the Market Analysis in my plan. Use this as a base outline for yours, and add to it as much as you see fit for your concept.

THE RESTAURANT INDUSTRY

- Discuss the state of the industry. What are the current challenges and the challenges ahead? What is the socio-economic or political climate? What businesses are thriving and suffering in the current climate? What sectors have seen the most growth in recent times? Is the growth sustainable?

CONSUMER TRENDS

- What is the current mood of consumers? How have their tastes/priorities changed or remained consistent? What are the trends that are here to stay? What do your customers value? Will this change if the economy changes?

SITUATION ANALYSIS

- What are the specific demographics of the city that your restaurant will be in? What is the size of the population, the largest—age population group, the average income, household type (singles, families, couples), white- or blue-collar population, education level, racial mix, the number of eating/drinking establishments.

COUNTY MARKET MIX & DEMOGRAPHIC

- The company I hired included a county demographic profile. This is useful if you plan on pulling customers from all parts of your county, especially for restaurants located in the suburbs, where many of the patrons have to drive to the restaurant. Otherwise, a restaurant located in a city will primarily depend on customers living in its own neighborhood.

RESTAURANT PROFILE AND TRENDS

- Again, these statistics were gathered by the marketing company I hired. This kind of information can be found in trade magazines such as *Specialty Food Magazine* and *Restaurant News*. Statistics include the age and income groups that are more likely to partake in leisure activities, frequent coffee bars, go to nightclubs, buy gourmet food, pay more for organic food. The information that you gather should support the concept that you're proposing.

COMPETITION

- Create a top list of establishments offering the most similar products and services that you offer. Identify their strengths and weaknesses. These can include location, menu offering, forms of entertainment, service, prices, ambience, visibility etc.

COMPETITIVE ADVANTAGE/POSITIONING

- Taking into account all of what your competitors are offering, cite what gives your restaurant its competitive advantage. You should be asking yourself, "What will make my restaurant important to the lives of my customers?" This question forces you to look beyond surface advantages such as "the first to offer authentic Mexican food" or "the only place offering jazz entertainment." While these are valid considerations to the need of your restaurant, they are not enough for your restaurant to be sustainable in a market that demands a more fulfilling experience.

ADVERTISING & MEDIA STRATEGY

- List the potential media outlets you will use to get the word out. This can include the online social media and mobile text messaging. Whatever you choose, it should be in line with your target market and should be measurable. If you place an ad, put a coupon or a special code word for the people to redeem so that you can quantify the effectiveness of your advertisement. Marketing is a top-line expense. Measure the return of your investment with any marketing expenditure.

- Create a plan of the actions you intend to take. And stick to it. Marketing is the most important function of any business.

- Incorporate a rewards club for your restaurant. Hire an outside company that specializes in this. If you don't have the budget to hire one yet, you can start out with a simple sign-up form that asks your guests for their birth date, e-mail address, mailing address, and comments. In return for their information, give them a gift certificate for your restaurant. You can do this even before opening by setting up a simple Web site with an opt-in form asking them for this information. This is the group you will nurture and will give you the most out of your marketing dollars because it will include the ones who are most interested in your restaurant.

THINGS TO REMEMBER

Here is a useful checklist of things to remember when developing your market analysis:

- Location – community traffic patterns, accessibility, visibility, surrounding neighborhood, parking availability, sign visibility

- Menu – theme, variety and selection, signature items, price range and value, beverage service

- Food quality – taste, presentation, portion size, consistency

- Service – days open, hours of operation, service style, quality of service, speed of service, extra service offered

- General information – Seating capacity, number of customers by meal period, entertainment

FINANCIAL PLAN

Know your numbers. Every business, no matter how noble the cause, boils down to numbers. Equity investors want to know how much money they're going to make and how fast. Lenders want to know when they will be paid back. Address both concerns with equal emphasis. You have yet to know how your business will be financed, and it could end up being a combination of debt and equity investment.

Your financial plan is almost completely hypothetical (unless you already have history selling your product/service), from the prices that you will charge to the volume that you will generate. Even the amount you need for funding is a guess. Granted, they're educated and informed guesses. But you are still making up numbers that you hope will be close to what you actually need and realize. This may feel awkward at first. But there are simple ways to make your numbers more tangible.

Start with an existing business that is close to what you want to do and observe the prices it is charging. Calculate the average price for an appetizer, entrée and desserts. What is the average price of a drink? What is the most popular item and how much does it cost? Count how many people you see in the place in a period of time; it could be an hour or a few hours. This is the same guerilla-style research that you will be doing when creating your concept. Take it even further by finding out what that restaurant's monthly utility bill is. If you don't have a way to determine that figure, ask everyone you know whether they know someone who owns a food and beverage establishment. Our degree of separation is a lot less than six. You will get an answer a lot faster than you may antici-pate. And of course, you have all the market research you've been compiling from the trade shows, magazines, etc.; and using the contacts you've made, call potential vendors and ask how much equipment and inventory cost. They have experience with helping restaurants open, and can even give you entire costs of construc-tion and opening inventory amounts. Ask which clients of theirs started small and what tips they may have for you to do the same. People are generous. Ask.

REVENUE MODEL

This section reveals the revenues you expect to generate from selling your core products and/or services. You can project down to the first weeks and months of opening to what you expect to make in year five. If you're going to sell food and beverages, estimate an average check for both categories. Estimate the daily volume, average it out for the week and multiply it for the month and then the year. It could look like this:

Average food check = $9.00

Number of customers a day, taking into account busier days of the week (volume) = 85

Weekly volume = 595 (85 x 7 days/week)

Weekly sales = $5,355.00 ($9.00 x 595)

Monthly sales = $21,420.00 ($5,355.00 x 4 weeks)

First year sales = $257,040.00 ($21,420.00 x 12 months)

It's a fair assumption that prices will increase over time. So for the second to fifth year, estimate what your average checks will be and calculate the expected revenue.

Year	Average Food Check	Average Beverage Check	Sales*
1	$9.00	$3.50	$357,000
2	$9.50	$4.00	$385,560
3	$10.00	$4.50	$414,120
4	$11.00	$5	$456,960
5	$12.00	$6	$514,080

*Based on weekly volume of 595

Profit & Loss Statement: Make a study of what makes up a profit and loss statement for a restaurant. I recommend the book *Uniform System of Accounts for Restaurants* (by the National Restaurant Association). All of the statement categories, such as General & Administration and Employee Benefits are described at length. You'll see what costs belong under each category and understand how the percentages are calculated. The percentages are helpful especially when you have no idea what a category may cost you. For example, Repairs & Maintenance will be difficult to forecast (although the more used equipment you have, the more likely it will give you problems), so take the average percentage of this category and multiply it by the total sales you estimate. The same can go for other categories that you find difficult to forecast. This is what a monthly P&L statement could look like based on the above scenario:

INCOME STATEMENT - Year 1		
Sales	**Amount $**	**%**
Food	$257,040	72%
Beverage	$99,960	28%
Total Sales	**$357,000**	**100%**
Cost of Goods Sold		
Food	$64,260	25%
Beverage	$14,994	15%
Total COGS	**$79,254**	**22%**
Gross Profit		
Food	$192,780	75%
Beverage	$84,966	85%
Total Gross Profit	**$277,746**	**79%**
Operating Expenses		
Salaries & Wages	$85,680	24%
Employee Benefits	$17,850	5%
Occupancy Costs	$35,700	10%
Direct Operating Expenses	$21,420	6%
Music & Entertainment	$14,280	4%
Utility Services	$17,850	5%
Marketing	$17,850	5%
Depreciation	$10,710	3%
General & Administrative	$17,850	5%
Repairs & Maintenance	$7,140	2%
Other Income	($2,856)	-(0.8%)
Total Operating Expenses	**$243,474**	**68%**
Operating Income	**$34,272**	**9.6%**
Interest	$17,850	5%
Income before Income Taxes	$16,422	4.6%
Income Taxes	$4,927	30%
Net Income or Loss	$11,495	3.2%
Retained Earnings, Period Begin	-	-
Less Dividends	$8,211	2.3%
Retained Earnings, Period End	**$3,284**	**0.9%**

FUNDING

Another forecast will be the amount of money you need to open and operate your business. Based on your concept, make a list of what you need to make the vision come true. From the refrigerators to the silverware, what are all the things you need to open your doors? This list can easily get long simply because fantasizing our dream place is fun. But this is where so many restaurant projects go wrong. Even if you secure a million-dollar investment, force yourself to prioritize what's most important to your guests.

Write down everything imaginable you're going to need. Create a simple spreadsheet and go down the list of the people, services, and materials. Call a law firm and ask for fee projections. Do the same with a plumber and an electrician. You can easily find out the cost of permits and licensing. By visiting furniture stores and restaurant supply places, you can get an idea of what dining chairs go for, the price of ranges and hoods, tableware, utensils, and your uniforms. Is real silverware an absolute must for your guests? Or can stainless steel be used with no adverse effect to the guest experience? How much is rent? How many months will it take you to build out?

Document the money you spend on the development of your business. A few dollars here and there can add up. The investment that you'll be making will not only be used for tax purposes, but to also reveal that you've used your own money to develop your business idea. It shows your vested interest and belief in your plan. And the feeling of self-reliance will add to your growing sense of confidence.

By the time I found funding for my restaurant/bar, my own investment amounted to more than $20,000. Most of this was for small purchases that accrued over the two years that I pursued my business plan. After I calculated this number, I knew that there would be no turning back. It was both frightening and empowering.

The final investment that I thought I needed for my business came out to $357,600. In my plan, I outlined that amount from the following categories:

Services	$27,500
Permits	$1,150
Leasehold Improvements	$43,000
Furniture, Fixtures, Equipment	$68,000
Pre-Opening Expense	$4,000
Liquor License	$70,000
Food and Beverage Inventory	$15,000
Working Capital	$25,000
Three Months Operating Capital	$100,000
Telephone Installation & Deposits	$500
Utility Deposits	$950
Insurance Deposit	$2,500
Total Start-Up Costs	**$357,600**

I ended up raising *a lot* less than the amount I thought I needed. By the time I opened, my bank account balance was zero. I was in a predicament that every business textbook, expert, and common wisdom warned against. Not only was I under-funded, with no cash reserve, but I was walking into an inevitable fight against the City of Jersey City to rewrite an antiquated law destined to hurt my business from day one.

But money doesn't reign supreme. Neither does the status quo. Deep down, we have resources far more valuable and much more powerful — resources waiting for us to awaken to them, to use for our desires, with the confidence and courage to know that they will not fail us. Chapter 6 takes us further into this idea.

PAYMENT SCHEDULE

I've seen many variations of a payback model for investors. You really are bound only by your imagination. A great benefit to you would be to research many examples of deal structures and payment schedules that have worked for others. The temptation is to paint a rosy picture to appeal to investors. While this may reel them in, it will also set the stage of what they expect from you. Whatever you claim the investor will see in return will set an expectation of you and your business. The better approach is to balance optimism with caution. Appeal to investors who are willing to grow with you, to ride the ups and downs of a start up and have patience with their money. If a bank ends up being your investor, agree to terms that achieve these same objectives. Honor your needs as a young business that needs its chance to grow.

I based my payback module on splitting net income after taxes every quarter. I claimed that the investors would receive 90 percent of income after taxes and the company would keep 10 percent. I also claimed that investors would be completely paid back by the second quarter of the second year. At the time of writing this book, my restaurant is going into its seventh year and the investors have not been paid back as planned. They have been patient but in hindsight, I would have done a few things differently relative to the financial relationship with my investors.

First, I would have made a point to pay them back immediately and consistently after opening – no matter how small that payment would have been. The feeling of having money back in their hands, on a consistent basis, goes far to relieving angst and preserving a sense of security.

Second, I would have accounted for the underfunding of the restaurant and foresaw the need to reinvest money from the business back into it. I would have created different case scenarios and what our options could be based on the situation. I offered a worst- case scenario where the liquor license would be sold to recover most of the investments. But I also should have included scenarios that weren't as severe, but still unexpected.

I would have been diligent about tracking our actual numbers relative to the forecasted numbers, creating clarity, and managing expectations more efficiently. And I would have *consistently* communicated with my investors once to twice a month. When communication is lacking, assumptions get in the way and create the potential for problems in the relationship.

ASSUMPTIONS

In this section, list the assumptions that you've made to arrive at your numbers. It's useful for your own reference if ever you're asked, "How did you arrive at that number?" The following questions will help outline the kinds of assumptions pertaining to your financial statements:

FOOD & BEVERAGE SALES

- What constitutes food sales? What constitutes beverage sales? (If you're a restaurant, soda/coffee/juice are considered food. If you're a coffee shop serving sandwiches, coffee is your beverage.)

- If you plan on increasing prices, by how much (dollar or percentage amount)? When (every quarter, twice a year, the beginning of every year)?

- Do you have an average price increase?

- How do you plan on achieving your forecasted sales besides increase in price? It could be services such as catering or extreme marketing.

EXPENSES

- Do you have targeted percentage costs, such as maintaining a 30% food cost or a 5% marketing cost?

- What are your variable expenses?

- How is depreciation being accounted for?

- Are there incremental costs, such as delivery charges?

- What is the sales tax percentage?

- What is the payroll taxes percentage?

- What is the corporate income tax rate? Is there a minimum corporate income tax?

- How have you accounted for the cost of living adjustment? What is the inflation rate you're assuming?

LOAN

If you were to acquire a loan, what could the interest rate be?

APPENDICES

This section typically contains the facts and figures that support the content of your business plan. The temptation here is to fill it up with fluffy charts and graphs that lack impact. Whatever information you choose to highlight and back up your case should be relevant, pertinent, and credible.

The types of information can be: demographics, industry trends, news articles, market research results, pro-forma statements, list of start-up costs, list of investments made.

SUPPORTING DOCUMENTS

I used this final section for official documents exhibiting the due diligence that was done. For instance, one of the first steps I took upon finding my location was writing a letter to the director of zoning for the city, asking him to answer *in writing* whether my location was zoned for a restaurant. I did the same for the liquor license that my landlord had for sale. I wrote the New Jersey Division of Alcoholic Beverage Control to confirm that the license was "clean" and free of citations and tax liabilities. I gathered such letters and put them in this section as compelling proof.

The documents in this section can be whatever is uniquely important to your situation: zoning letter, liquor license check, Building Department approval of plans, insurance coverage, resume, letter from vendor partners (perhaps you secured an exclusive relationship with a crucial vendor, ask them for a letter that supports your claim).

Insurance coverage comes into the picture early in your planning stage because you will need to know how much to budget for it. Your landlord will ask for a certificate of insurance upon signing your lease. My husband Robert, who is in the restaurant insurance business, has told me many stories of restaurant deals going bad from overlooking important insurance requirements. Hire a broker that specializes in restaurant insurance. This person will know the unique risks that you will need protection for and all the coverages necessary.

Gathering these types of documents will help secure your plans and avoid surprises in the planning stages.

Chapter 6:

BEING RESOURCE-FULL

oney tops the list when we think of resources. Most of the decisions in our lives are based on us judging whether we have the money or do not have the money to do what we want. In this section, I dare you to put money at the bottom of that list of resources. I dare you to stop judging your life's circumstances. And I dare you to uncover the power you have to create the business you want, the life you desire, with resources that money cannot buy.

When raising money, the local lending community and the Small Business Administration rejected me. American Express was the only company to approve me for a couple of thousand dollars. Every person who showed interest in privately investing never did. But I still got my chance at business despite the odds, and to successfully grow it in unfavorable circumstances.

YOUR LIST OF RESOURCES

At some point, your restaurant will obviously need the money to get it open. But what if the money doesn't come as fast as you think it would? What if the source you expected to get it from denies it to you? What if you are afraid to part with your own money? What if you are freshly out of college, with no money, no credit, no equity, but so badly want to have your own place? How far will you pursue your dream? Will you commit to making it happen, no matter what?

I ask these questions because most of us think that money is the answer to our problems, that money will make it easier to pursue our business. But time and again, having money does not guarantee restaurant success. Failed celebrity restaurants are a testament to that. And having no money is no guarantee for restaurant failure, either. My story exemplifies it. Money is a tool, among many tools. When we stop putting so much value on money, other resources appear ready for our taking.

The great news is that even after your business opens, these resources remain key ingredients to your success. There is one caveat to using them — they will work for you in proportion to your willingness to use them.

INNER RESOURCES

In a 2005 study called *Why Restaurants Fail*, Dr. H.G. Parsa, currently the chair of food service and lodging management at the Rosen College of Hospitality Management, University of Central Florida, revealed that "the restaurant failure rate is affected more by internal factors than by external factors." While the internal factors comprised operational elements such as strategy, product, management, financial, marketing, type of ownership and culture, personal characteristics and goals were cited as the "guiding force" of a restaurant's environment and ultimately its success.

Using a sample of 20 successful independent restaurateurs who operated a full-service establishment for a minimum of five years and 20 failed restaurateurs who operated the same types of places, the research team uncovered no example of a restaurant failing due to external forces. Those external forces included competition, legal and political, economic, demographic, technological, social and cultural, suppliers, customers, and regulatory agencies.

"Failure seemed to stem in large part from an inability or *unwillingness* to give the business sufficient attention, whether due to a lack of time, passion or knowledge," the study found. Other excuses that the research cited included "demand of labor and time...no longer willing to make family sacrifices...lack of concept." The list is long. But these are just effects from the one true cause: not taking responsibility.

What it boils down to is that we do not have anyone or anything but ourselves to blame if the business fails. These findings are astounding for the person ready to take personal responsibility for his or her success. And perhaps this is where the dilemma lies. Are we willing to be responsible for our own actions and ask more of ourselves, day in and day out?

SELF-HONESTY

Self-honesty starts with asking yourself difficult questions and being courageous enough to answer them truthfully. A good place to start is here:

Ask yourself what is the worst that can happen, and can you live with that outcome? What you'll discover are the things that matter most in your life, right now. If you're afraid of looking like a failure to your friends and family, then what matters most to you is the opinion of others. If you're afraid of losing your money and never recovering it again, then what matters most to you is the feeling of security. If you fear failing, what matters more is protecting your self-esteem.

But fears don't just surface from thinking of the worst that can happen. Fears also appear at the thought of succeeding. We say to ourselves, "Who do I think I am... for wanting my own restaurant... for wanting to be successful... for thinking I am worthy of what I want?" The effect of such defeating thoughts becomes a case of self-sabotage, with most of the victims being unaware of what they are doing.

You could possibly find yourself having everything you need – the money, the resources and the passion – to create the restaurant you want. But if the fear of success is lingering in your subconscious, then you will effectively find a way to ruin your plans. And you will succeed in self-sabotage because of your underlying *beliefs* that you don't deserve what you want.

Confronting what is holding you back gives you the opportunity to let it go.

PATIENCE

Having patience is not waiting to see what happens. It is working toward your goal while knowing that it will happen in due time. As nature shows us, there is a gestation period, a time it takes for an idea to take physical form. But motion must be set to make this transformation. A seed has to be planted. An idea must be acted on.

Opening my restaurant hinged on the idea that I could change the Jersey City law that restricted the hours that restaurants could serve alcohol. The restriction was imposed upon a small section in the downtown area and spearheaded by an equally small group of neighborhood activists. During construction of the restaurant, these people would pay me visits, reminding me that if my intention was to change the city law, that I could count it lost.

It took two years, over 1,000 petitions, three mayors, and one unseated councilman to change the law. And every day it took patience to see it through. My opposition did their best to protect the law they helped create. The police received constant calls to check on my restaurant. There was a period when every Friday, 15 minutes before closing time, I could count on ABC officers being at the entrance of the business.

But while their focus was on intimidation, I focused on the positive steps I could take. I talked to patrons about the ordinance, solicited their support, and asked for a signed petition. I asked for help from everyone around me. And it came. In due time, I had my chance at City Hall. With a caucus full of supporters and a speech that is still talked about, my motion to change Jersey City law happened in October 2005.

When we want something so badly, it seems we can't have it fast enough. But I kept my focus on managing my business under those circumstances, while doing something every day that took me one step closer to changing it.

When the desired result seems so far from your reach, focus on the things that are within your immediate control. Small accomplishments go a long way in keeping you motivated to reach the bigger goal. And as time passes, you will discover the patience that you may have not known you had.

FAITH

There is no denying it – having and keeping your faith when everything you see tells you otherwise is one of the hardest things a human being can do. Faith is believing your thought to a point that you are not denying that belief. Faith is a gift that we are all endowed with. But as in any of the resources available to us, internal or external, faith is available to us to the extent that we use it. When you wholeheartedly and completely accept the thoughts you tell yourself, then your faith is working for you.

DECISION

You need to make the kind of decision where there is no turning back. You can zig and zag, but you must continue forward and never retract from the decision that you've made. Faith and decision go hand in hand. The strength of one depends on the strength of the other.

You know what you want. Decide once and for all that you will get it. Yes, you may have to make corrections to your plans along the way. Yes, sticking with your decision will demand enormous strength of character. And yes, you will get overwhelmed at the daunting task that lies before you. But it is this place of discomfort that your greatest rewards are found. In time, what was once your personal struggle will become your source of strength.

I've heard business speakers and mentors compare making a decision to burning bridges, with a hint of the willingness to risk it all. While I do believe that fortune goes to the bold, a bold action is relative to the person. Declaring your business plans to your family with conviction (and no concern to their reaction) can be a very bold step for you. Calling vendors and introducing yourself as the president of your company can be a very bold step for you. Leaving your job to pursue your passion can be another bold step. It all depends on the person making the move.

Burning the bridge doesn't have to be making an overtly shocking, life-altering move. It can be taking many small bold steps. It's not about making a statement, it's about the joy of knowing what you want and making the decisions to get you there.

ENERGY

Inertia is the single biggest obstacle for any entrepreneur. Mix it with doubt and discouragement, and many end up with an abandoned business idea. The fact remains, nothing happens until something moves. Wherever you are right now, you have the chance to start on your restaurant project. And if you are well into it, and come across unforeseen obstacles, there is still something you can do. Whether it's coming to a creative solution around the obstacle or shifting your focus to another area of your business, action can always be taken.

Our energy is in our control. We have somehow bought into the idea that our energy is dictated by our schedule, our responsibilities, and ongoing circumstances. We want more time, thinking that we will find more energy. But if we dare to think differently, we would find that we've been in control all along. Energy is as much a state of mind as it is a physical state.

You have complete control of your thinking, and therefore exert control over your energy. You can talk yourself into having energy by sheer mental determination. We see examples of this when people, especially athletes, get their second wind. These bursts of energy come from a renewed state of mind. In the moments when you tell yourself that you "don't feel like it," know that inertia is creeping in. Instantly after thinking it, your body wants to slow down. And then you find the excuses to justify your lack of energy. This is the road that leads to unfulfilled desires and constant frustration. Break the cycle.

TIME

Perhaps the most untapped resource we have is our time. For many of us, our actions are dictated by our emotions. And unless we feel good about our endeavor, unless we are optimistic, full of energy, and committed to what we set out to accomplish, we get sidetracked and our time gets wasted. There is no making up for the time that we lose, so guard it. And use it.

When I was juggling working a 9-5 job as an assistant event planner, I couldn't wait to get home to work on my business. I had the job for only three months before being let go, but during that time I managed to finish most of the content of my business plan. I saw how much I could get accomplished just by focusing on one area of the plan. Whenever I would get ahead of myself and want to achieve the results faster, I took time out from doing work and did nothing. Sometimes this is the best use of our time. But no matter if I got nothing done, my time was still purposeful.

HUMAN RESOURCES

Other resources that you can turn to are other people's expertise and support. These can come from your family, friends, acquaintances, and even strangers. People are generous. For us to experience their generosity, we must be willing to ask for it. People who can help want to help. We have been conditioned to not bother people or learn to do it ourselves. Or that people are busy and don't have time for us. This just isn't true.

Whenever someone has asked me business questions (and some have been as intimate as asking how profitable we are, or how much rent we pay) that come from a sincere desire to learn from me, I have never hesitated to give that person the information he or she asked for. I've had the same experience being on the receiving end. When I've had to seek other people who knew more than me in certain areas of the restaurant business, I've been met with generous outpouring of wisdom.

You can reciprocate people's help by bartering or spreading the word on their kindness. I've had to ask friends for architectural advice, then offered free dinner and drinks when the restaurant opened. They knew that no money was to be had by lending me a hand, but that didn't stop them. And neither should you feel guilty for people's generosity. The best way to honor them is to happily accept what they are so generously offering.

And then there are people in your life who know how to bring out the best of you. They are the ones who have an endless supply of kind words, but who also aren't afraid to give you tough love when you need it. These are the people who don't just tell you what you want to hear, but who are secure being themselves, and have the gift to transfer that security to you.

CREATIVE RESOURCES

We are all creative centers from which our lives and those around us are being constantly influenced. Creativity is not a special talent reserved for the artistic type. At any time, we all have the power to tap into our creative side. Every time we solve a problem, we are being creative. When we make a presentation and turn it into a sale, we have used our creativity. The fact that we have an imagination is a testament to our creative nature. The difference lies in the degree that we exercise it.

As you move along the process of creating your business, there will be plenty of moments when you might not get what you want. Sadly for many, if this scenario happens enough times they will quit their pursuit and blame it on the difficulty that got in their way. Now that I have the ability to look back and trace my steps, I can attest that every obstacle was perfect in the way it was presented. In most of those instances, I had to use my creativity to move past the challenge and learn the lesson that was waiting for me. Many times, I just had to reinvent my attitude about the situation. Frustration is best overcome by your imagination. Being creative is really a way of life. It is being consciously aware of the choices we can make at every turn. And how we can turn every situation advantageous to ourselves.

MONEY

It would be absurd not to include money to our list of resources. But it's my hope that you now have a broader understanding of how money really can be put at the bottom of that list. Money may give some people the luxury to forego a lot of the resources cited above. But it wouldn't make them any smarter about their money. Nor would it equip them to succeed if the money disappears. It happens all the time. Million-dollar projects go bust within a matter of months. And many are left wondering what happened. Many of them get a losing start by simply going over budget. And this happens because most over rely on what money *can* buy, and therefore don't use all of the other resources that they had at their disposal, for little to no cost.

If you find yourself not yet having the money to start your restaurant, then look to your other resources to keep you going. Time is a big one. For the *time being*, you can work a second job to fund other parts of your business that need funding. I had second and third jobs as a waitress for a sushi restaurant, and as an on-call server for a couple of catering companies in New York City. From these I was able to pay for blueprints and a score of other items necessary for the business.

If traditional lending institutions keep turning you down, look to the human resources that you have. Your family, friends, and acquaintances are the next logical group to tap into. Ask everyone you know. Don't predetermine who you think will most likely say yes to lending you money. You never know who may be surprisingly generous with their money. From my experience, especially in the very beginning, acquaintances to the point of being almost strangers pulled through for me in times when I was short for rent money. And one such person lent money for multiple months of rent. The bulk of the money ended up coming from my immediate family, but not until a year into the project. For 12 months I had to tap into my other resources.

At the heart of what I've shared thus far is my desire for you to have an enduring belief that there are ways for you to make your restaurant happen. The next few chapters of the book will go into practical detail on how to build your restaurant from scratch. The assumption I take is that (A) you want to start simple to avoid risking it all or (B) you have to start simple because of a limited budget, and eventually want to grow it over time. My scenario was both A and B. I believe that anyone wishing to open his or her first restaurant should aim to begin simply.

Chapter 7:

BUILDING THE SPACE

I t's no secret that the restaurant industry works on small margins. Some of the best operators in New York City operate at an average of 10 to 15 percent net profit. With such a tight return on investment, any new restaurant should aim to open with as little cost as possible. Of course, low cost does not equal cheap. There is a dramatic difference between the two that I will cover later in this chapter.

What I'm referring to is avoiding what Dr. H.G. Parsa calls the *Taj Mahal syndrome,* a common trap that would-be restaurateurs often fall into. The scenario goes like this: The restaurateur makes building the perfect restaurant his ultimate goal, uses most of his money for construction, and thinks that his job is finished when the doors open. But this is not a sound business approach. If you take into consideration what Dr. Parsa cites as a 10-year average life span of a restaurant, and add the fact that the industry margins average no more than 15 percent, a restaurant has very little time to make its money back.

Instead of attempting to build a restaurant shrine, restaurateurs should aim to create a business that best represents their intended concepts, stretch every dollar in their budgets, and leave plenty of room to adapt and grow the business over time. This is the essence of taking a simple approach. This makes even more sense as our society continues to shift in trends, tastes and preferences at a drop of a hat. What were once normal, lavish restaurant interiors suddenly became gaudy and over-the-top when the economy turned south. These are the risks of going into business, but we can control many variables — a major variable being the final cost of development for the project.

Determining whether a project is low cost is obviously relative, since the amount of money in question depends on the person with the money. A lot of money to one person can be pocket change to another. So a good place to start is by looking at how much you plan to make in sales per year. Professor Parsa cites a 1-to-1 ratio of annual sales to cost of investment. If you plan to make $1 million per year, you should plan to invest $1 million into the restaurant.

If we use the 1-to-1 ratio as our benchmark, then we should strive to spend less than that standard amount of investment. If you plan to make $100,000 annually, then strive to need less than that in investment. I projected to make $250,000 my first year, and my investment amounted to $150,000, which $70,000 of it was used to pay for the liquor license.

I was left with $80,000 to build my restaurant from scratch. By the time I opened, there were many things left to be desired. But the main thing was, I opened, gave the business the opportunity to receive cash flow, and managed that cash to grow the business over time. With only one new investment of $50,000, the business now grosses close to $1 million annually.

SETTING UP THE RESTAURANT

Before I go into detail on how I built my restaurant on such a small budget, it's important for me to point out the situation I was setting up for myself. When choosing your final location or outlet for your place, remember that this is the most important time for you to set up your business for success.

Location

The space was located in a commercial street in the middle of the downtown district of Jersey City. It was not the financial district of downtown, which has its challenges with nighttime business. The location of my space was in a neighborhood business and residential district. There was life on the streets at all times of the day and throughout the week. Major transportation was steps away, and New York City was a 10-minute train ride away.

The area was still up and coming. There were plans for a new high-rise development and streetscape renovations as the town was seeing an influx of young professionals, families, and New York City transplants. But the condition of the neighborhood at the time made it evident that there was some time to go before the aesthetics changed for the better. I capitalized on that fact when negotiating the lease terms. But my landlord was a fair man, and had already taken that into consideration.

There was yet another change that Jersey City needed to make, though it had not planned on it until I made it my mission. There was a small downtown section that the city deemed Restaurant Row. Oddly enough, that same area was restricted by an ordinance that prohibited restaurants and bars from serving alcohol past 11 p.m. on weekdays and no later than midnight on weekends. The ordinance was pushed by a neighborhood association, which argued that if the city was going to promote that area as the Restaurant Row of Jersey City, the residents ran the risk of a loud and late-night drinking scene. The city accepted that demand and put a stipulation on its own effort to attract more restaurants. My restaurant was located right on the main commercial street of Restaurant Row. And by the time I moved in, there was only one existing restaurant on the row since the city's initiative eight years prior.

My landlord, Steve, broke the news to me during one of our meetings over our lease agreement. It appeared to be a major setback and I asked for time to rethink the situation that I was about to get into. Steve had the conviction that the ordinance could be changed. But the person who had to initiate that change would have to be me — a 24-year-old, freshly out of college, taking her first stab at the restaurant business in a town notorious for its unscrupulous politics.

I did take that stab. But I knew that if the laws were to be changed, it was going to take some time. I negotiated my lease terms some more.

Rent

Steve initially offered three months of free rent at $3,000 per month for the first year. I negotiated six months of free rent and a reduced rent of $2,500 for the first year and a half. He structured my rent roll so that it never saw a dramatic increase until more than halfway into the lease. And the lease was set for 20 years with a five-year renewable.

When you're negotiating rent, be assertive and agreeable with your landlord. Know what you want and be confident about getting it. A good landlord wants his tenant to succeed and is sensitive that a new business needs time to get it off the ground. Remind your potential landlord of that. Appeal to his understanding and support for his new tenant. If you find the landlord being strict with what he wants and refusing to acknowledge your concerns as a new business, then reconsider the space. Find a landlord who is just as eager to see you succeed as he is to collect rent.

Hometown

This is a major advantage I had from the beginning. I knew that my chances of succeeding would be greater in the town I grew up in. I knew the culture, I knew the people, and I understood their desires. I saw the dramatic changes that were happening along the waterfront throughout my years in college. And by the time I graduated, it was clear that Jersey City was ready for a neighborhood place with a New York City vibe.

Understanding the mores of a town is crucial for your business. Even big cities have varying cultures in different parts of town.

Some communities may have certain loyalties and if you come in as an unfamiliar face, you could be viewed as an outsider who doesn't understand their way of life. But there are so many ways to prevent this sort of resistance. So don't let that be a deterrent for you as you find a location. Just know that those types of conflicts are possible and plan on ways to integrate your business into the community.

CONSTRUCTION OF THE RESTAURANT

The construction phase of your restaurant is a fun and frustrating experience. Your anticipation is high, but the inevitable delays and challenges in constructing your place will also be in high frequency. Prepare yourself to manage both your money and your emotions during this exciting time of your business venture.

Tip: Create a spreadsheet that lists everything you know and can possibly imagine needing for the construction of your restaurant. Some items will be of more priority than others, such as plumbing work versus a computer point of sale system (the technology can wait, but your pipes cannot). Itemize each product and service you need and budget wisely. Evaluate every buying decision you make.

PLUMBING AND ELECTRICAL

Plumbing and electrical work must be done by professionals. When doing your restaurant on a budget, don't cut corners in these areas. You will be better off in the future by hiring competent professionals to construct important pipe and electrical work.

Be diligent in choosing a plumber and electrician. Ask for references from other commercial spaces they've done and call the owners. Ask them about their experience, if anything went wrong, and how efficient the contractors were with their time. I went through five plumbers. My first plumber did most of the work, but when he decided that he was paid enough for the work he did, he left the job and offered to finish it for more money. Always keep enough of a carrot on a stick for contractors. Be sure that the final payment is a sizable amount for them to want to finish the job.

On the other hand, I had a great experience with my electrician. He was a reputable contractor, conscious of my budget, finished the work, and even let me pay him over time. But he was also the father of a friend from grade school. Most of the time, these types of connections with people benefit you in ways that this did for me. However, I do know restaurateurs who were taken advantage of by friends in the business. Everyone's experience is different, so the main thing is to know the scenarios that can happen.

BE YOUR OWN GENERAL CONTRACTOR

In most municipalities, you can be your own general contractor through a simple purchase of a bond indemnifying the town. This process took less than a day and for a mere few hundred dollars, I became a licensed general contractor. The place to ask is your town's building department. If you don't know where that is, call the city hall.

When I thought of hiring a general contractor to handle the entire construction of the restaurant, I was repeatedly given misinformation. I was told that I had to hire a G.C., that the building department won't cooperate with anyone but the G.C.'s they knew, that my papers had to be passed by certain people for the restaurant to be approved. These scare tactics worked in the beginning, and so I did initially hire a general contractor for the project. After I gave him $2,000, he disappeared, and I later found out that he had a gambling problem.

When I went to the building department, I discovered that my paperwork was never submitted by the G.C. I hired. I told the director that the G.C. ran off with my money, and the director assigned one of the inspectors to oversee my project. I was taken under the inspector's wings and before I left, I had someone who cared about me at the building department.

Being your own G.C. carries a tremendous amount of responsibility, much of which I didn't know going into it. But I had no choice at the time, because of my small budget and the fact that I was already a couple thousand dollars behind. A general contractor orchestrates the entire construction. You rely on his expertise in completing the job on time, managing other contractors such as the plumber, electrician, carpenter, mason etc., supplying the building materials, and getting the job approved by the building department to get your certificate of occupancy. This work comes at an expense. You will have to decide, based on your budget and unique circumstances, if it's in your best interest to hire one or do it yourself.

CARPENTERS, ENGINEERS AND OTHER PROFESSIONALS

I hired a competent carpenter to do the framing work for major structures such as our kitchen wall and bar counter. I also had him teach us how to do the framing, and with the help of my brother and friends, we wound up finishing what the carpenter started. We also did most of the drywall and plastering work.

However, when it comes to manipulating building structures such as beams and supports, an engineer must be hired to ensure the integrity of the building and your ultimate safety. We had to raise two doorways in the basement that rested on beams in the building. So we set aside a definite budget to hiring a structural engineer.

Your architect should be a trusted consultant. This person knows exactly which professionals need to be hired to complete the work properly. But our architect was a vanilla box-type architect who produced blueprints for the sole purpose of meeting the building code and played no part in the construction. I would advise to not follow my footsteps in this regard. A good architect will save you much time and money in the long run.

LEVERAGE HARDWARE CHAIN STORES

As general contractor, I had to complete the tasks that that person would normally handle, one of which was to supply the building materials. By this time, I had already made many visits to Home Depot when I was doing my initial market research. I familiarized myself with the different kinds of wood available, different paint finishes, and creative ways to build a restaurant on a budget. Much of the information I learned by asking the people working at Home Depot and other people I knew to be knowledgeable on the subject.

Apply for a commercial credit card from a hardware chain store such as Home Depot or Lowe's. This will help with your cash flow. Instead of paying for all of the materials at once, you have the ability to pay it off over time. If you have partners, ask the person with the best credit to apply for the business. You want to get the highest credit limit possible. I had my brother Jerome apply for the business and we were given an initial limit of $4,500. We were able to do a lot with that line of credit. Put your money and your imagination to work.

BUILDING MATERIALS:

Drywall - we purchased all of the drywall, fire-rated, water-proof and in different thicknesses, we needed for the construction and repair of walls. Building codes must be adhered to. If you are your own G.C., check with your building department. Try to have a go-to person at the department so your questions can be answered faster.

Wood - We purchased everything from the birch that we used for the bar counter, to the 4 x 4s used to build the kitchen wall, to the 24-inch square plywood we used for the table tops. I used better grains of wood for the areas that the guests would see and feel.

Paint - Choosing the paint color was easy. It had to be primarily white since the restaurant was to be a gallery as well. But I had to experiment with different finishes for the bar counter and tabletops to make sure that the paint could withstand spills and constant contact.

Cement - the bathroom floor was cemented, and part of the basement floor had to be leveled out with cement. This is a fairly inexpensive material and there are so many creative ways to use it. I considered making the bar out of cement, but chose wood so that it could be painted white.

Tile - I didn't use much tile except for the kitchen floor and behind the bar. Tiling should be done by someone with experience. You can get creative with mosaic tiles, and use unusual pieces as tile work. I once saw a bar made out of beer bottles cemented in a mosaic pattern. Many artists work with tiles, so consider finding one you can commission.

Soundproof material - used in walls and ceilings.

Miscellaneous materials - spackle, sandpaper, nails, screws, dimmers, grout, metal frames, telephone cords, doors, hinges, brushes... everything imaginable.

Equipment - electrical saws, drills, spackling tools, electric sander, power gun, etc.

Rental equipment - professional paint sprayer for the ceiling, floor sander, and truck to transport large and heavy materials.

RESTAURANT EQUIPMENT

There are certain equipment that you don't need to buy new. As a rule of thumb, if the equipment does not have a motor and doesn't visually impact the guest, then don't buy it new. Sinks, racks, and stainless steel counter tops for the kitchen are such items. These pieces don't rely on a motor and chances are will be situated in places where the guest won't see or touch them. If, however, you design an open kitchen and the aesthetics are important, then consider buying them new or looking almost new.

Gas equipment is usually better to buy used than electrical is. For example, gas fryers have a longer life than the electrical fryers. Refrigeration is a very important consideration. The last thing you want is for a motor to blow out on a refrigerator and have your food spoil. I suggest that you use new refrigerators for your food storage and used refrigerators for beverage storage. Most beverages won't go bad with a change in temperature. Plus, I find that the older refrigerators can be visually more interesting and can add a certain flair to the look and feel of your concept. If you know someone who repairs equipment, bring that person along when scouting for used equipment.

A word of caution – as I mentioned before, there is a big difference being low-cost and cheap or skimpy. Certain beverage companies will provide free refrigerators to operators that carry their brand. I highly recommend not having these refrigerators on display. Most are cheap and skimpy looking, do nothing to enhance the ambience, and instantly commercialize your place.

FURNITURE AND FIXTURES

Choose your furniture and fixtures with a keen sense of awareness of the *effect* that you want to achieve. Textures, patterns, colors, and designs all evoke different feelings and perceptions from the guest. Vinyl has a cold feeling, while velvet conjures warmth. Colorful mosaic tile will evoke a different feeling from minimal monotone tiles. Orange is supposed to spur appetite, while the color green soothes. Spend every chance you get to observe the choices that other successful restaurants have made in designing their space. My favorite French bistro in New York City purposely constructed its booth seating to look as if it's been worn in. Trinkets and French countryside objects add to the charm and uniqueness of the space. These details matter and together will create the ambience and vibe of your restaurant.

Invest your time, focus, and interest in developing the look and feel of your place. Out of food, service and ambience – ambience is the most important to your guest. Go to furniture supply stores and ask for swatches of different fabrics and colors. Bring them home and *sit* on your options for as long as you can until you develop the instinctive knowledge of which choices to make. In the beginning, I thought of having dark furniture because in all of my experiences going to lounges in New York, the color and mood tended to always be dark. But as I sat on the idea for a while, the more I started to question if that was the right color choice for my concept. The fact that my restaurant was also going to be a gallery weighed heavily on the color scheme. And came to the conclusion that having a white space for the art to attract the attention was important to the integrity of a gallery. In the end, I decided to make all of the furniture, including the tabletops and bar counter, in the off-white color.

Another important consideration is the combination of new and used furniture. You may find that your concept does not have the sensibility for old furniture. It could be a concept of the future and references to the past may just confuse the nature of your place. But if you do have room to incorporate used furniture, I highly recommend doing so. Granted, not all used furniture is created and preserved equally, so it's going to take a discerning eye. Your goal is to choose smart pieces that evoke a feeling of familiarity and uniqueness. Know your balance of used versus new furniture. Random pieces that are out of harmony with one another can confuse your desired look and feel. But depending on your concept, such as my favorite French bistro, many random pieces can work well in achieving the charm and character of your restaurant.

Take pictures of your favorite places, cut out magazine pictures of restaurants or items that strike your interest, and start making a mental log of what attracts you and the reasons why. Evaluate what you like and determine what feelings they evoke. For instance, if you are drawn to glass – glass plates, glass surfaces, glass sculptures etc. – understand that that material has a cold feel to it. The opposite experience would be having wooden materials that evoke warmth and comfort.

There are many places to search for your furniture and fixtures. Many major cities have a specific area where restaurant supply stores are located. If your town has one, this would be a good place to start your search. These stores should have catalogs for you to search to get more inspiration. The idea for my dining chairs came about by visiting a chair store and seeing a bucket chair that was meant to be paired with a high base, and then seeing a standard height chair base to match it with. It was a look that was out of the ordinary and an inexpensive option to avant-garde furniture design. Other sources for you to consider are the following:

- Furniture mail-order catalogs

- Flea markets

- Public auctions and estate sales

- Junkyards – this is where some of my favorite pieces were found. We bought old school bus seats and used them as our lounge seats in the front of the restaurant. Patrons loved it and we achieved a good balance of new and used furniture. We bought four bus seats that sat 8-10 people at $10 per seat.

- Online resources – eBay, Craigslist, local swap sites, clearance sites. All of our lighting fixtures were purchased from an online lighting store that was having a clearance sale on extra-large spotlights and the halogen lamps to go with them.

- Antiques stores, second-hand stores such as Salvation Army.

- Ikea – my only caution with using Ikea is to avoid using too many of their items, especially their large furniture pieces, as they aren't constructed for commercial use. And while many people are used to seeing restaurants use Ikea's inexpensive wares, I recommend using Ikea for smaller items and wares such as candleholders, glass pitchers, salt and pepper shakers, etc. These pieces are necessary items for your restaurant, but don't make a huge impact on the look and feel of it.

- Trade shows – here you can locate custom furniture makers, importers, and distributors of all sorts of pieces for your restaurant.

- Home Depot – I purchased 30 half-inch-thick, 24 x 24-inch wide square plywood pieces, painted them white, and used them for my initial tabletops. I eventually replaced them with thicker tabletops with white veneer.

- Local furniture upholstery place – these stores sometimes have furniture that they've restored available for sale. I used them to reupholster retro barber chairs that were being thrown away by a local barbershop.

- Do-it-yourself – if you're inclined to make your own furniture, look into doing it. Our bench seating was homemade. I bought white vinyl upholstery and foam from a wholesale store, used a professional staple gun that I rented from Home Depot and created our own bench seating.

LIQUOR LICENSES AND VENDORS

According to John Bodnovich from the American Beverage Licensees organization, obtaining a license to serve alcohol in a restaurant is often one of the more challenging aspects to the start-up process. The reasons for this include local or state license limits, state bureaucracy, and local citizen opposition. Many restaurants depend on their alcohol sales to add cushion to their tight profit on food. The ability or inability to obtain a liquor license often determines the fate of a restaurant project. If you decide to have your restaurant serve alcohol, do extensive research on how to obtain a license and get answers directly from the people who issue them.

After Prohibition was repealed, each state either adopted or resumed control over its own liquor laws. Because of this autonomy, each state's laws can be completely different from the others'. And to take it one step further, each county and municipality within each state can also have varying liquor laws. However, each state does have an Alcohol Beverage Control division that oversees the enforcement of these laws. If you want to serve liquor in your restaurant, do your research well in advance. Call or visit your local ABC office to find out what the city ordinances and state laws are that could affect your business plans. You can find a complete list of state ABC offices at www.restaurantfromscratch.com/ABCOffices.

States are divided into two general classifications: "control" or "license" states. There are 18 control states that act as the sole wholesaler of distilled spirits and retailers in other ways. Restaurants in those states have to buy their liquor inventory from state liquor stores. There are 32 license states that do not act as the direct wholesaler, but issue and regulate licenses to industry distributors within the state. Restaurants order liquor from distributors (independent of the state) doing business in that state. To see the list of "control" states in the United States, go to www.restaurantfromscratch.com/ControlStates.

Some states no longer issue liquor licenses; and in those states the only way to obtain one is through the purchase of an existing license from another owner. One town might have its licenses going for $100,000, while another town in the same state can have its licenses going for a $1 million. Then there are states that still issue licenses, but on a city level; those licenses might be controlled by zoning ordinances and community approval. Each town can vary greatly in the days and hours that alcohol is permitted to be served. Some towns prohibit the sale of alcohol on Sundays. Some go so far as banning liquor altogether.

With such varying degrees of control, I recommend reaching out to your state or local ABC office. From there you should be able to get most of your liquor law questions answered. Liquor associations are another great resource. You can ask them questions more focused on your business, as these associations usually promote or protect the interest of liquor-license owners. When I was doing my research, I contacted the New Jersey Liquor Beverage Association and with its help received a list of the state's beer, liquor, and wine distributors. I became a member, which enabled me to stay abreast of the laws directly affecting my business. Contact the American Beverage Licensees (ablusa.org) to get more information on liquor associations available in your state. And before moving forward with obtaining your liquor license, consult a lawyer who specializes in this field. Liquor associations should have these legal contacts.

Go to www.restaurantfromscratch.com/liquorlicense for more resources on this important topic.

FOOD VENDORS

Trade shows are a good place to find food vendors. There you'll find most of what you will need for your menu. The more specialty dishes you plan on offering, the more you're going to have to source purveyors that specialize in distributing certain ingredients.

The National Restaurant Association's annual restaurant show in Chicago is an all-encompassing show. The exhibition floor runs the gamut of restaurant equipment suppliers, food vendors, industry technology, special services, and more. You can also attend special workshops and presentations from experts in the industry. The expanse of the show can get overwhelming. But for any show, I recommend having a set of goals that you want to accomplish so that your time and energy are focused.

Another show I recommend is the Fancy Food Show that travels to large cities in the East and West Coasts. This food-focused show is geared mainly for retail shops. But most shops are prepared to supply restaurants and will sell in bulk quantities. The show is especially helpful in getting a pulse on the food trends.

Check with the conference centers nearest you to see what shows they may have coming up. Trade magazines are another good source for upcoming industry events. Some of these publications even sponsor their own trade shows. Commit to attending at least a couple of shows per year. Being exposed to the latest trends, products, and services will keep you and your business relevant.

TYPES OF VENDORS

- Broadline distributors — these types of distributors offer everything across the board. Think of them as the one-stop shopping source. Their hope is that you will buy most, if not all, of your products from them. They sell perishable and non-perishable items. The convenience of using them for all of your needs is attractive, but be aware. I've found that they tend to mark up paper products much higher than a specialized distributor would. They know that most companies that exclusively sell such items usually have a high order requirement. You will have to weigh the benefits versus the cost when it comes to situations as these. If you do end up using one or two broadline distributors for everything, use that to negotiate competitive pricing.

- Specialty distributors – these suppliers specialize in a specific category of goods. The advantage is that you can expect superior products and, at times, better services than broadline distributors. Some specialty food purveyors have exclusive selling rights to products, especially if they come from a small farm or operation. Conscious diners who want to know the source of their food are on the rise. And oftentimes your ability to trace and acknowledge your food source allows you to command higher prices with little to no buyer resistance. Specialty distributors sell items exclusively such as exotic vegetables, fine meats, ethnic products, paper products, bread, etc.

- Cash and carry – these places sell an array of products for restaurants, but require that they be picked up and carried out with you. They usually have a restaurant's basic needs and don't specialize in any product category. Because they don't deliver, their prices can be 10 percent (or more, depending on the product) cheaper than broadline distributors and specialty suppliers. Jetro, Restaurant Depot, Costco and other discount stores fall under the cash and carry category of purveyors.

- Artisan retailers/wholesalers – there has been a great revival of artisan food purveyors that dedicate their business to producing fine, and oftentimes limited, goods. They can be a local cheese shop, charcuterie shop, or others that fit with the artisan approach to specialized production. These retailers usually supply to the public, and many supply restaurants at wholesale prices. Specialty distributors frequently represent a number of these artisan producers and help streamline the distribution to food service operations.

VENDOR DYNAMICS

Your vendors are your partners. The success of their businesses is predicated on the success of their clients. Use this synergy to your benefit. Ask for their support, especially as you first start out. They have marketing expenses that are designed to help their accounts. Some distributors have an in-house executive chef to help clients with menu testings in the company kitchen. The larger distributors are more likely to have this service than the smaller ones. Others can help you with the cost of menu design and production. When I first opened, my liquor distributors supplied the menu covers, table tents, and print work for the bar. Whenever dealing with alcohol, check with your local and state Alcohol Beverage Control to see what the liquor distributors are legally allowed to supply to their clients.

Some purveyors are more motivated to help their accounts than others. So don't wait for them to initiate offering their services to you. Actively seek it. Tell them before you open an account with them that you expect a level of participation and support to help your business grow. They should be continuously providing samples of new products, informing you of trends affecting your business, inviting you to food and beverage tastings.

DISCOUNTS

Your vendors are in business to help your business. This relationship should be of mutual respect and open communication. In the beginning you may have to build that confidence and trust before being issued extended credit. You may be asked to pay COD (cash on delivery) to create a history of payments to the company. In due time, you should be able to ask for credit, although I advise asking for credit from the very beginning. Many of them will extend you credit, so ask.

Vendors reward clients who pay fast and so expect to get a discount on your invoices when you do so. For example, if a distributor extends you a 30-day credit, and you pay it in 20, the company may automatically give you a 5 percent discount. The rule of thumb is the faster you pay, the higher the discount. If you're not told of this from the company, solicit it. These tiny discounts go straight to your bottom line and add up.

IDEAS TO GET STARTED

By the time you finish your business plan, do your research, and have what you need lined up. You may still encounter unforeseen challenges. The wisdom is in still taking *action* toward what you want. While this section is not meant to get you to think small, its purpose is to plant some ideas on how you can still get started in the event that obstacles come your way. Again, start with what you truly want and tweak that as you see necessary and as you *go*.

RENT A RESTAURANT

Displaced chefs have taken their creative skills to the dining room by renting out existing restaurants. These chefs strike deals with restaurant owners and become their temporary tenant. For a certain number of days per week, during the times when the restaurant is usually closed or slow, the tenant chef sets up shop and calls the restaurant by a different name. The chef can get creative, as guests patronizing this type of concept tend to be adventurous. These arrangements are temporary, and can be taken to other restaurant sites with owners who are open to the idea.

If you are employed by a restaurant that has not tapped into other dayparts, such as lunch or brunch, or other outlets for revenues, such as catering and delivery, you may be the person to initiate building that business. This is a great way to test your entrepreneurial spirit with a low-cost and low-risk endeavor.

WINDOW-FRONT

I first saw this many years ago in New York City's Chinatown. An elderly woman was enclosed in a small box attached to a building, and through a window-front, was selling small mooncakes filled with red bean. Recently, but in a more posh part of town, I saw a similar operation with a woman selling cupcakes. From the back of a corner retail store, the cupcake lady sells her homemade cupcakes in six different flavors. While we don't know what they pay in rent or the logistical problems they may cope with, we can assume that such an operation doesn't require much capital and is a proactive way to get started.

STREET VENDING

These operations can be street-corner hot dog carts, an ice cream truck selling sushi to go, or street-fair vending. Street vending has its own set of challenges, but is nonetheless a way to make a small start. Vending licenses can be difficult to obtain, especially for mobile trucks. The weather poses a major influence on your ability to do business. And because transactions are mainly in cash, and can be handled by one person, the issue of having trustworthy employees is magnified. But when you're starting out, chances are you will be that person working until you expand the business to afford hired help.

HOME-BASED CATERING

My first job out of college was for an off-premise catering company in New York City, doing millions in annual sales. The owner started by catering small dinner parties in private residences. It was just her and her best friend/partner in the beginning. And in less than a decade the company grew to become a major catering facility that not only did off-premise events, but also managed and operated restaurants in institutions such as museums and hotels.

By complying with your local health department codes, you should obtain a certificate allowing you to use your home kitchen to make food products for public consumption. State and city regulations can vary, so check with your local health department. From there, you have the ability to cater off-premise parties and make food products for retail operations or online distribution.

THINK BIGGER

Sometimes people think so small (because of the belief that that is where they *should* start) that they find it difficult to get started. When goals are too small, the thrill of the challenge and motivation suffers. If you find yourself in this position, stop what you're doing. Change your focus on where you think you should be starting and focus on where you want to start. These are two very different states of mind. Follow your inspiration, and your way will be made easier.

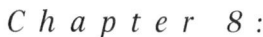

Chapter 8:

MARKETING

Marketing is one of my favorite functions in business because it is the area that we can use and best display our creativity. Art shows, film screenings, field trips, beer clubs, and cooking classes are just some of the marketing that I have done for my restaurant. While it is a lot of fun, the bottom line is that marketing must produce a profit for your business while enhancing the experience for your guests.

People have an insatiable need for new experiences. Being offered the same thing, the same way, all the time will eventually bore your customers. Marketing is the secret ingredient. It adds excitement to the routine of your restaurant. It is as important to your business as flavor is to food.

Marketing is the *legs* of your concept. The time to think about marketing is when the concept is being created. Based on your concept, what interest can you create so your customers want to patronize your place, repeatedly? Keeping the restaurant authentic to its purpose, meaningful to its audience, and constant with its impact is the start of effective marketing.

AUTHENTICITY

Being authentic in your marketing boils down to this: using the voice that is distinctly and naturally yours. Every business has one; and as hard as some try to imitate others, consumers have an intuitive sense of the difference between them. This is because at the heart of authenticity is the unique source of inspiration that the business was founded on. To find your voice, look at what inspired your restaurant in the first place.

The idea of LITM was to bring new experiences to the neighborhood it served. The burgeoning art scene in Jersey City was a major source of inspiration. LITM sought to connect the art and artists to the general public, in a social atmosphere of a restaurant. Art and providing new experiences would become the authentic nature of my restaurant, and our voice would have a tone of creative excitement.

The nature of your restaurant will be different. A person may want to provide artisan- style pizza using only the freshest ingredients. The nature of this pizzeria could be unconventional, yet honest and simple. The voice stems from this nature. The better you understand the premise or mission of your restaurant, the easier your voice will come to you.

RELEVANCE

There can be a fine line between marketing and creating gimmicks. What I find to be the true measure between the two is relevance. Whatever marketing tool you use – whether it's a coupon or special event – must be relevant to your concept and to the values of your customers.

A friend of my husband's at one time suggested we do a ladies night with a promotional raffle giving away Coach bags. This had gimmick written all over it. Even though people love freebies, this would have been completely irrelevant to our concept and customers. First, the women patrons that we attract view themselves as being independent, with their own sense of style. A large group of them would have to identify with the Coach brand of handbags before catching their interest. Second, commercial handbags have no relevance to the restaurant's concept. If they were one-of-a-kind pieces made by a local artist, then that would have had more relevance than a mass-produced Coach bag. And singling out a group of patrons, ladies or men, goes against our value of bringing everyone together.

But staying relevant goes beyond avoiding hokey promotions. Knowing what is at the top of mind for your customers is of major importance. Every one of us has a host of priorities occupying our mind at any given time. And no matter how authentic your marketing message is, if it doesn't appeal to what's going on inside the person's head, then your efforts will be wasted. If economic instability occupies a period of time, then financial security becomes a top-of-mind concern for many people. To stay relevant to guests' needs *and* fears, marketing promotions should emphasize price-value and extraordinary service. People pay for great service and are more likely to be loyal if priced at a value.

Be informed of the news in your community, country, and around the world. Stay abreast of industry news, but search beyond restaurant-specific information. Seek other industries, such as technology, entertainment, environment, and wherever else your curiosity takes you. Listen to the comments of your patrons. Search for trends in what they may be asking for. If you have yet to open, listen to the critiques that your friends make of other places. Information comes in many forms and is readily available when you are being attentive.

CONSISTENCY

Marketing takes discipline. The fact is, many restaurants will not invest the time and attention to the marketing needed to sustain and grow their business. Many will sit and wait for people to walk in, instead of actively creating ways to entice them. Many will try occasional advertisements and some will participate in a citywide restaurant week event. But not many will think outside of these marketing norms. Nor will many plan out each week of every month with new events that can be fun and memorable for their customers.

Marketing builds relationships through constant communication. As with any relationship, it takes time, attention, and commitment. It is a give-and-take. You give customers reasons to come to your place with the goal of them taking your offer. This back-and-forth never ends. If the communication stops or becomes inconsistent, the relationship with your customers suffers. They need your constant attention.

At the other end of communication is consistent execution. Do you do what you say you are going to do? The worst offense a business owner can commit in marketing is to fail to execute the intended results. Whatever you claim in your marketing should be backed up by the execution of it. And if you know that there are going to be limits or restrictions to your event, then make that known. Every marketing effort creates an expectation from your guests. Manage their expectations from start to finish. This is where the trust is built with your customers.

PLANNING

Marketing is an area where I learned as I went. Besides the art gallery as part of the concept, I did not have a thought-out plan for marketing the business. The monthly art shows were popular from the start and drew many art-related events. But if you asked me if I had a plan for all of our events, the answer is, I didn't. We were typical of a restaurant with a haphazard approach to marketing. We waited for major holidays such as Halloween and Valentine's Day, did occasional tie-ins with movies and art cocktails such as when *The Da Vinci Code* came out, had a political poster-making contest during one of the presidential campaigns, and other such events. We were not short of them, but lacked the skill to measure and maximize participation. We were relying solely on word-of-mouth advertising and hoped that enough people knew what was happening at LITM.

I was going into my third year in business when I saw us hitting a sales plateau. I wanted to make business better and knew that something had to change. I began searching for answers. I was a member of an online community for restaurant owners, and one day read an article about birthday marketing. This marked the start of our marketing system. I immersed myself into understanding the marketing process, and discovered that the best form of marketing is what is known as *direct-response marketing*.

Before learning about direct-response marketing, I had invested a lot of time and money toward image/brand marketing. This is the kind of advertising that we see most of in magazines, commercials, billboards, and other mainstream media. You can spot image marketing/advertising because they all lack the ability to track the results of the campaign. Fashion ads, Super Bowl commercials, and million-dollar logo campaigns are all examples of image marketing that claim to do a lot for brand recognition, but fail to tell you just how much more money it has made you.

Direct-response marketing is a different practice. It knows whom you are targeting and tracks how much response your marketing generated. It allows you to measure the return on investment for every marketing dollar you spend. Catalog mailers are an example of direct-response marketing. These companies acquired your name from a list of similar buyers, sent you a marketing piece (the catalog), probably gave you an irresistible offer with your first purchase, and are able to track any sale that you generate for their business.

This section is an introduction to the direct-response marketing that I have learned through the years. Direct-response marketing is a study on its own. The more you understand the process, the better off your business will be. Everything that I share and recommend doing, I have done myself. You will not be disappointed with the results. A year after I adopted these marketing techniques, sales increased by 40 percent. And year after year, they continue to grow.

Learning about marketing is not going to benefit you unless you implement the marketing. Marketing how-to books are everywhere. The problem isn't lack of information; it's in the execution. As with most endeavors, the time will come when you've learned as much as you can and the only thing left to do is take action.

MAILING LIST

The first lesson I learned was this: How are customers supposed to know what your restaurant is doing if you have no way of contacting them? This was hard to swallow. I had already been in business for almost three years when I realized that I had no mailing list. Don't make the same mistake. Create your list even before you open and never stop compiling it once you are in business.

People must have a compelling reason to give their personal information (especially today, when consumers know how valuable their information is to companies). You will be asking for: name, address, e-mail, birthday, and anniversary. You can ask for more information, but you want to make it simple for the customer. In return, offer a desirable gift to the people who sign up. It could be a $25 gift certificate for food and drinks (liquor law permitting), a free dessert or appetizer, or any other prize that your customers consider valuable. The more generous your offer, the more people will sign up.

Example of Mailing List Form

Become a member

FREE meals, exclusive offers & fun stuff. Plus it's
FREE to join! Complete & submit to server or drop box

Name_____

Email_____

Address_____

City_____State_____Zip_____

Ph_____Birthday (m/d) _____

Seriously fun!
We Promise!

Even before your business opens, you can begin to build your e-mail list with current technology such as mobile text marketing or online social networking sites. With mobile text marketing, plaster your storefront with signs showing a code number people can text to receive a freebie, such as an entrée, once you open. When people text your code, their number is automatically stored in your database. The information you gather will just be mobile phone numbers, but you still have a captive and interested audience. When they eventually patronize your place, you can then ask them to fill out a complete mailing list form, offering them more freebies.

If you want to acquire a mailing list overnight, hire a company that specializes in selling names of people in your area who fit your demographic profile. This is what catalog companies do. It is equivalent to cold-calling customers, so expect more resistance. This means you may have to offer even better deals and free products to gain their confidence in patronizing your business. Start with a small list, and if the results prove worthy, buy more names.

COPYWRITING

In direct marketing, there are different levels of copywriting from the very simple to complex. But they all share one goal – to get your customers to participate. Participation could mean having them buy, sign up, make a reservation, or any other action you want them to take.

There is a formula to follow that will make it easier for you, especially in the beginning. Here is a list of the elements needed in your copy, by order of appearance:

1. **Headline** – this is the most important part of your copy, because it's the first content that your audience reads. The headline is usually a short sentence that grabs their attention immediately.

2. **Subheadline** – the subheadline expands on the headline and must also entice the reader to continue reading the copy.

3. **Body** – this is where the whole picture is usually presented, where you can explain your offer, gain their trust, build your credibility, describe your services, tell your story, etc. Every sentence must keep your readers' interest and increase the likelihood of their participation.

4. **Call to action** – this is where you tell your reader what to do next. People want instructions on what to do when they are interested. Make it clear and easy for them to do.

5. **Expiration date** – an offer must expire for it to be taken seriously at the present moment. A sense of urgency compels people to take action.

These elements are sufficient to produce simple marketing pieces such as postcards or small ads. But as you dig deeper into direct-response marketing, you will soon discover that there are a lot more tools that you can and should use.

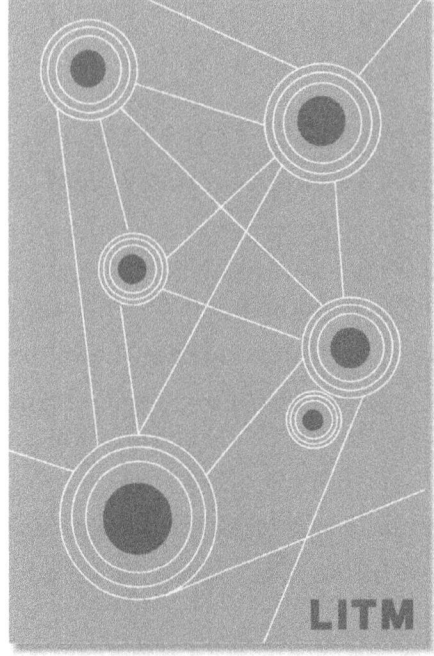

◄ Example of brand marketing: relies on imagery, conveys no message.

▼ Another example of brand marketing: emphasis on logo, message is vague.

OTHER COPYWRITING TECHNIQUES

Every copywriting element is designed to increase the response from your customers. The general rule of thumb is, the bigger the price tag, the more copy you have to write. And copy doesn't just mean words. It involves techniques that increase the effectiveness of your writing. Here is a list of such techniques:

A. **"P.S."** – at the end of your letter, adding a *P.S.* note has been proven to increase results. Some readers skim through a letter and oftentimes will jump to the bottom to get the point of your message.

B. **Picture** – an image speaks a thousand words. Whatever picture you use must be relevant to your copy. Add a content-rich caption underneath the picture because most people will read that first to decide whether the entire message is worth reading.

C. **Guarantee** – a guarantee helps break down the resistance to buy or use your offer. Most people are skeptical of offers, even free offers, because of the notorious restrictions or conditions that businesses often tag with the free offer. If you're giving away a $10 gift certificate, write, "With no strings attached" to alleviate their skepticism. Another rule of thumb is the higher the price for your product, the better the guarantee has to be to reduce the buyer's resistance. As a side note, you should be confident in your product and service before offering a complete-satisfaction guarantee. Guarantees must be upheld to preserve the trust of your patrons and the reputation of your business.

D. Testimonials – if you already have a track record of happy customers, then ask them to write a testimonial to use for your marketing. You may want to reward the people writing the testimonial for taking the time to do it and for their consent in your use of it. Testimonials are highly credible because they are comments from your customer's peers. Be sure to include the person's full name and city and state. It adds to the credibility of the statement.

E. Attention grabbers – these are usually throwaway items such as cheap plastic toys, knick-knacks, candy, golf balls, and other items that will grab the reader's attention. These are particularly useful if you are mailing letters in envelopes. The bulge that these items create by being stuffed in the envelope will get the recipient curious enough to open it.

F. Premiums – these are prizes that reward the person for participating in your marketing offer. There are usually multiple prizes that the person can choose from. An example would be a letter telling your customers about your special three-course pumpkin menu being offered in October. In this letter you may ask them to purchase a dinner ticket in advance, and to reward them for doing so, you offer them one of three premiums: a free pumpkin cocktail, a $10 gift certificate for future use, or a surprise course in the pumpkin dinner. The goal is for you to get people to commit to your event ahead of time and collect payment on it as soon as possible.

G. Credibility – if you win an award or receive a favorable review from a restaurant association or food magazine, market that fact. If you appear in the media, such as TV or radio, share that fact.

H. Personalized font – use a font that is easy to read, but one that also looks personal. You can even create a font using your own handwriting from Fontifier.com. Scribbles in the form of asterisks, circling words, underlining, and exclamation points are other touches that help make your copy look personal. Just be sure that the scribbles are an enhancement and don't interfere with the legibility.

I. Stamp placement – stamps placed at an angle or upside down have been shown to increase responses. People are so used to generic junk mail that they can easily spot them in their pile of mail. If you use a special-edition stamp and tilt its placement on the postcard or envelope, that will help set it apart from the junk mail.

GUEST FUNNEL

A business sustains itself through a positive cash flow. Restaurants compensate for their low-average transactions by doing volume. And to do volume, a restaurant needs a constant influx of customers. This is why restaurants cannot afford to be passive with their marketing. Effective, measurable and constant marketing is the best guarantee to a steady flow of business.

The following hourglass diagram best describes the process of acquiring new customers and keeping existing customers. These are two distinct groups that are marketed in different ways. Some ways to attract new customers include mailings to households that fit your demographic profile, advertisements in local newspapers and community Web sites, social media, and traditional media publicity. New customers must be compelled to give your restaurant a try. The ultimate goal of your marketing effort is to graduate as many new customers as possible into becoming regulars of your restaurant. Your regulars will be the source for most of your business. By knowing who they are and how to contact them, you will experience immediate results for your bottom line by having a simple and effective marketing system.

The top of the hourglass is wide open and represents the process of getting as many people through your door as possible. Buyers' resistance is the highest at this point because people are not familiar with your business and are apprehensive about trying something new. It is at this level where you must give people a compelling reason to give your restaurant a try. If you just opened, you will naturally get an influx of curious guests. Don't let any of them leave without asking them to join your rewards club. These offers can range from gift certificates in small amounts, free food, free drinks, and anything perceived as high value by your customers but low risk to you. You won't know which offer is the most effective until you try different ideas and track the results.

As you move down the hourglass, the pool of customers you started with at the top begins to shrink. This is the filtering process. At this stage, you are asking for customers to sign up to your in-house rewards program, VIP club, or whatever you decide to call it. The guests who are interested in your business and want to participate will separate themselves from the pool of new customers. The people who sign up are telling you that they are interested and are giving you permission to solicit their business. There is little to no sales resistance from your "club members."

HOURGLASS MARKETING MODEL

New Customers – high buyer's resistance

Sign up guests for rewards program. Build list of club members

Mail three-month marketing campaign to turn them into regulars

Restaurant newsletters

Regulars – low buyer's resistance

Exclusive events

Upsell

The offer to initially get people to join your club can be as simple as giving away a free appetizer. Ask as many people as possible to join. The larger the pool, the more people you will have as members. When someone joins, be sure that he or she receives what you promised. I recommend mailing the offer so that the recipients have a reason to come back to your restaurant. Don't offer the giveaway on the spot, because you risk collecting fictitious contact information. (But this isn't to say that instant giveaways should be ignored altogether. Immediate freebies can be beneficial in different scenarios.) The goal with your marketing is to create a habit in people to *think* of your place. Being on top of their minds increases the chance of them choosing your restaurant. These same customers will eventually turn into regulars, assuming that you deliver a consistently pleasant experience.

From the moment that a customer joins your list, the time imme-diately following is the most crucial in winning attention and nurturing repeat business. Mailing the free gift to the customers who join is your first follow-up marketing and is a crucial step in building their trust. And a few more follow-ups need to be done before you can confidently expect the customer to graduate into being part of the captive audience (the bottom half of the hour glass). To plan for this series of follow-ups, create a three-part marketing campaign that shares a common theme and is mailed within a three-month period or less. To illustrate, the following page shows the follow-up campaign I used for LITM for a number of years.

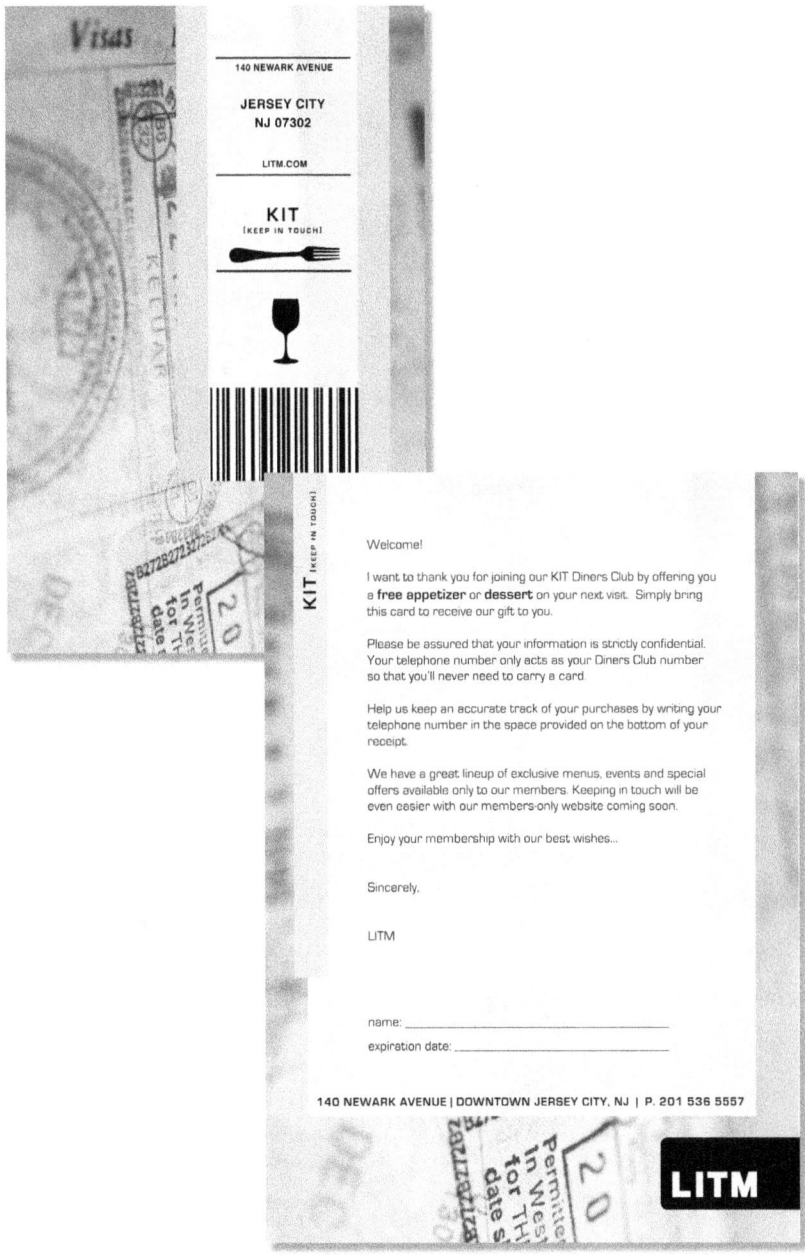

Our rewards program was first named, KIT (acronym for Keep In Touch). This was the first mailer that members received. It was for a free appetizer or dessert.

THREE-MONTH MARKETING CAMPAIGN

FREE PLATE of PASTA

Ciao!

I'm usually good at keeping secrets, but this one has to be told. The Last Supper was catered by LITM.

I tracked his lineage using all my connections. And it's true, Filippo Russo is a descendant of the master chef of that infamous meal.

One bite and you'll be convinced of the authenticity and creativity that only a Renaissance man can guarantee.

Use this card by

to receive a free half plate of pasta!

Ciao,

Leonardo

140 NEWARK AVE
DOWNTOWN JERSEY CITY
NEW JERSEY, 07302
P. 201 536 5557 | LITM.COM

LITM

I started to have more fun with our marketing and created a three-month postcard campaign of famous artists. The first month was Da Vinci offering a free pasta dish.

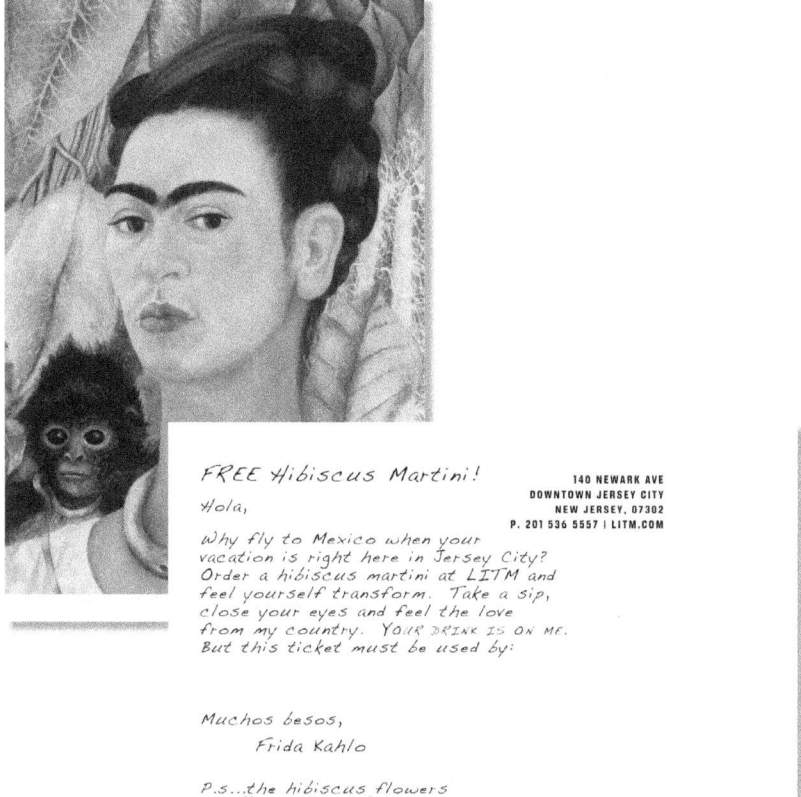

FREE Hibiscus Martini!

140 NEWARK AVE
DOWNTOWN JERSEY CITY
NEW JERSEY, 07302
P. 201 536 5557 | LITM.COM

Hola,

Why fly to Mexico when your
vacation is right here in Jersey City?
Order a hibiscus martini at LITM and
feel yourself transform. Take a sip,
close your eyes and feel the love
from my country. YOUR DRINK IS ON ME.
But this ticket must be used by:

Muchos besos,
    Frida Kahlo

P.s...the hibiscus flowers
are flown direct from
Mexico City to LITM!

LITM

The second month's postcard was from Frida, offering a free hibiscus martini.

FREE Messy Sundae!

Hey there,

140 NEWARK AVE
DOWNTOWN JERSEY CITY
NEW JERSEY, 07302
P. 201 536 5557 | LITM.COM

You gotta have the messy sundae
at LITM. It's so good that
i'm putting my name on it. You'll
know an artist made it - drips of
chocolate everywhere, layers of ice cream,
strokes of whip cream, splatters of nuts,
bananas and cherries. Come see a work of art!

Bring this card for
your FREE Van Gogh
messy sundae.
Come in before

Dank je,
Van Gogh

LITM

The third month's postcard was from Van Gogh offering a free messy sundae. Note that every postcard has a catchy headline, attention-holding copy and an expiration date. Plus, they were a lot of fun for our customers to receive.

The ultimate goal of this three-step follow-up process is to create a regular customer who *knows*, *likes* and *trusts* you. Mail your offers within a month from when they first join. The offers should be perceived as valuable and be easy to redeem. Avoid too many restrictions. Send your members three separate offers that are each one month apart, and track your results. You will see an increase in sales, and most of all, anything that your company sends out will be received with enthusiasm. You're giving before getting, so the reward of your generosity is having a captive audience that is excited about your business.

NEWSLETTER

You will have developed a relationship with your customers through the gifts you have mailed them. The next step is to nurture your relationship with your guests through the most effective marketing tool: the newsletter.

A newsletter is an opportunity for you to bond with your customers and at the same time promote your business. There is a science to the type of content to put into a newsletter that will increase readership. For one, the newsletter cannot be all about your business. Provide content that is useful to your customer and relevant to your restaurant. For example, you may want to write an article on holiday entertaining. It may talk about how to create a holiday menu and decorate a table. This doesn't directly promote your business, but it is still relevant. At the end of the article you could remind the reader that your restaurant does off-premise catering and include a phone number to place orders.

Talk about yourself in the newsletter. Include your family and pets. If you're going on vacation, tell them about it. If you just came back from one, put pictures of your trip. This is your chance to make a connection with your guests. They want to know the person who they're doing business with. People buy from people. They want to feel good about who they are spending their money with. Don't be afraid to get personal or talk about your values and what you believe in. Think about what you want your restaurant's role to be in the lives of your guests, and create your newsletter around that. Whatever you write should be guided by your sincerity and a desire to add to people's lives.

A cartoon and fun trivia are a must for your newsletter. They're easy to read and lighthearted. A coupon is another must. It entices people to at least peek at the newsletter and is a simple way for you to track reader participation.

Promote a two-way communication between you and your guests by including them in your newsletter. We featured a couple who had their first date at LITM and, at their one-year anniversary at the restaurant, got engaged. We took pictures of them and put them in our newsletter. You may introduce or highlight a guest each month and write about that person's career, hobbies, and favorite drink in your restaurant. Or you may run a contest and announce the winner on the newsletter. There are hundreds of ways to include your customers in the newsletter. Go to www.restaurantfromscratch.com/newsletter for more ideas.

The format of your newsletter will depend on what works for your guests. I had my restaurant's newsletter designed as an oversized color postcard. You can have yours in whatever format you desire – letter-size paper folded in half, legal-size paper in a trifold, or a magazine-style newsletter. I wanted to keep ours short but still full of the information necessary for a newsletter. The following is an example of one of our postcard newsletters.

Postcard Newsletter Sample –
October & March

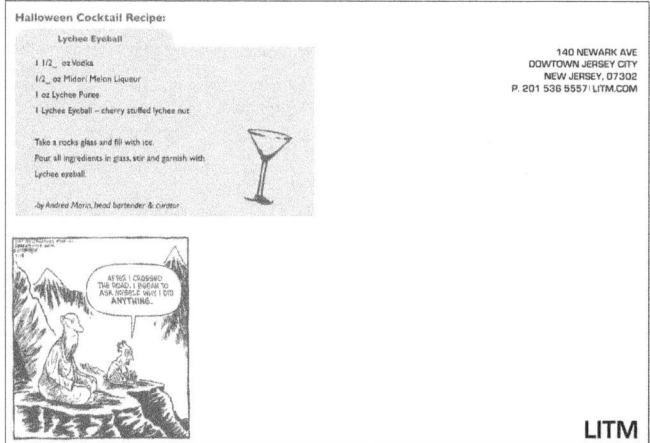

This was an October newsletter mailing. Note that it has all of the elements needed for a successful newsletter format.

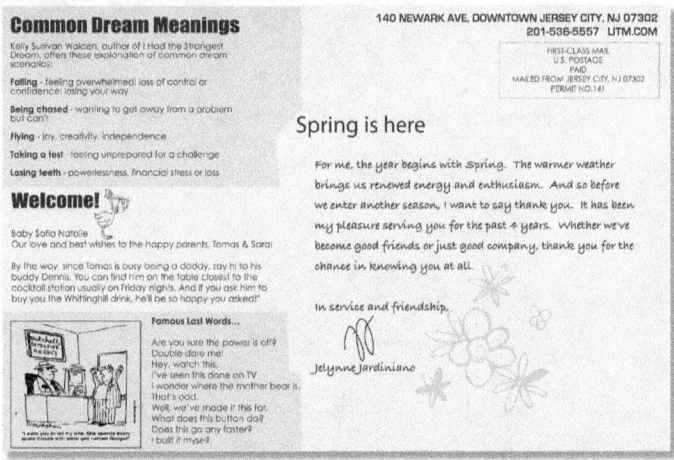

This is a March newsletter with an opening letter signed by me. Little touches like this can make a lasting impression on your guests.

Doing a monthly newsletter is time consuming. That fact is enough reason for restaurant owners to abandon the idea. But there are companies that create custom newsletters for your business. You typically work with a copywriter to decide on the content you want in the newsletter, and the company does the layout, design, printing, and even mailing. Go to www.restaurantfromscratch. com/newsletter for a list of newsletter companies.

ONLINE MARKETING

Technology has made it so easy for a business to market itself online. With a couple of clicks and little to no cost, your restaurant can have an immediate online presence. But the Internet requires constant communication from your company if you are to get noticed. However, whatever you communicate can be short, as long as it's consistent.

E-MAIL

It took me three years after opening my restaurant to collect my customers' e-mail addresses. I thought people didn't want to be bothered. I thought that it was intrusive to solicit people's contact information. I was afraid of communicating to them – what would I say, how would I say it, will they care? Those assumptions and self-doubt held me back all those years. Don't let them hold you back.

People want to be reached out to. People want to be informed. Yes, they are interested, and yes, they care. Otherwise, they wouldn't be giving you their information. If you have fears about writing to your guests, start with a quick note. Be consistent with it and build on your writing over time. Your guests will look forward to your e-mails because it is a message from the owner.

Use professional e-mail services for your e-mail marketing. The cost is minimal for the convenience it will give you. Of all the things to save your money on, do not skimp on this. Using free e-mail services from sites such as Google and Yahoo to send your restaurant's e-mails is a sure nightmare. Those sites limit the number of users that you can send to at once and can flag your e-mail as spam. With the anti-spam laws, you are almost required to have your e-mail subscribers confirm their subscription with an opt-in e-mail. One afternoon, a regular customer of mine expressed how annoyed he was by all the e-mails he was receiving from another bar in town. It turned out that the other bar had sent its e-mail via AOL, and a recipient of the e-mail had hit "reply all." That's all it took to start a string of unwanted replies to the entire list, and create a bunch of angry customers who demanded to be removed from the list. Go to www.restaurantfromscratch.com/proemail for a list of e-mail service companies.

WEBSITE

Your website has a great impact on how your restaurant will be perceived, especially by your prospective guests. The image that you portray online will be as important as the ambience that you create in the actual space. The site should accurately reflect the kind of experience that your guests should expect from your restaurant. And most of all, it should capture their interest.

Have your website work for you. Make it possible for visitors to your site to join your rewards program online. Add links to your social media pages and ask them to befriend or follow you. Have coupons downloadable from your site.

Think of your website as another marketing piece. It should grab their attention and make them take action. Highlight the events coming up and keep the content current. Your website is constantly working for you. But it will only attract customers to the extent that you keep it fresh and updated. And there is no such thing as a small detail that can be overlooked. Our Thursday daily special initially offered all-you-can eat mussels and frites. But the kitchen advised us to change the frites to bread, and so we did. We forgot to update the site and guests were still coming in expecting what was posted on the site.

You have many options in getting a website created. Companies that sell domain names, such as Godaddy.com, also offer services that creates your website. The best way to create one is to hire a local designer. This person should be familiar with your neighborhood and the personality of your restaurant.

Blogging

This is another medium that I avoided for years. My first encounter with blogs and online communities were complaints about us. I had an idea that the only people who took the time to blog or post comments were disgruntled and had nothing better to do with their time. So I decided that I never wanted to be like those online dramatists as I saw bloggers to be.

But I would eventually push my feelings aside and dissolve my bias. Around the time that I became knowledgeable about marketing, I couldn't avoid the topic of online marketing. Blogging was hailed as a great way for search engines to find your company and top search rankings. It was a great medium to connect to customers and foster two- way communication. Blogging is a great way to keep the interest of your customers.

I couldn't ignore blogs as much as I tried. So I stopped resisting and added one to our Web site. I started with caution at first, only writing about upcoming events. And then I slowly added bits of personal information like places I had just traveled to. And then I started to elaborate on those travels and came to discover that I liked blogging. I realized that I, too, could be just as opinionated as anyone else on the Internet and talk about what I am most passionate and qualified to write about – my business.

When creating your blog, try not to put pressure on your writing. Not everything you blog about has to be profound or even related to your business. Write for yourself and about what makes you happy, even if it means complaining.

One more point I want to make — I denied myself the opportunity to use this tool by my ignorance in thinking I was somehow getting back at the people who made complaints about us. This lesson isn't about blogs, but about going into areas where it hurts and confronting our fears. I had to confront my fear of being criticized. I felt threatened by bloggers who made mean comments, and feared that my writing would also be attacked. I eventually built up my courage and discovered that fears disappear the moment you decide you want them to.

SOCIAL MEDIA

Social media sites are a lot of fun, free, and a powerful marketing tool. After blogging, I joined the trend of social media and became a Facebook member. I got connected to people I saw every day and to people I hadn't seen in years. In a matter of a few weeks, I had a network of hundreds of friends to market to. These people already know, like, and trust you. Having contact with people you already have a relationship with gives your marketing an instant edge.

The preferred social media site may change over the years (having witnessed the rise and fall of such sites as Friendster and MySpace), but the lesson remains the same. Go where the people are. And join the conversation. For help with getting started with social media, go to www.restaurantfromscratch.com/socialmedia.

OPENING

H ave your marketing plan in order before you open. The weeks leading up to your opening will be an intense time. And during the first six months, you will be so involved in the day-to-day operations that marketing could easily be abandoned. Do not let this happen. Your business will grow by the strength of your marketing.

It took four months from the start of construction to our opening day. Even when that day came, I felt like I wasn't ready. I was just intent on getting income coming in and planned on having a grand opening weeks later. But I was so wrapped up in making every day better than the one before that the soft opening never lead to a grand celebration. I don't regret it.

In fact, I recommend forgoing a grand opening altogether. The usual course is to invite public figures, the media, and friends and families to a red-carpet ribbon-cutting ceremony. Events like these should be centered on your guests and not on people who may never show up again. Restaurants end up giving away their inventory, which they shouldn't do so early in their business life.

Instead, prepare your restaurant for a great soft opening. There will be many things to attend to, so the key is to stay organized and focused, and enjoy yourself. Opening your doors is just the beginning.

SOFT OPENING

The time between preparing for your soft opening and actually opening is a period of constant trial and error. Be patient with yourself and the outcome of your plans. Not everything will work out the way you hoped, but everything that does happen is pointing you in the right direction. Keep your eye on your vision and be open to what your environment is telling you.

PRE-SOFT OPENING:

- **Menu testing** – your business plan may have had a preliminary menu. Chances are that menu has changed or been tweaked by the time you are ready to open. I thought I was going to be a full-service restaurant from day one. But I had no budget for a kitchen operation, so the food had to wait.

  This is your chance to get the food and drinks just right. If you're a restaurant, testing is critical. Invite people whose opinions you respect for a pre-opening tasting. If you're solely a bar, like I was in the beginning, you have more flexibility with the menu testing. I was so focused on opening that I didn't even have a drink menu ready.

Menu testing not only involves tasting, but costing as well. By this time, you should have your vendors chosen and have a close estimate of what your cost of goods will be.

- **Hiring** – I took my time with this before opening and I still experienced high turnover. The problem I had was that I didn't know what I was looking for. I thought I was supposed to hire for experience, but I learned over time to hire for personality. If a candidate has both, even better. You know the experience you want your restaurant to provide for its guests. Hire people who will deliver that experience. Outline your values and expectations from the start. You want people to weed themselves out and attract those who identify themselves with your culture. The best way to find these people is to ask your star employees or customers to refer friends. This isn't fail-proof, but it's better than placing ads.

- **Training** – people will always remember how you made them feel. Define the experience that you want your guests to receive, write down your vision, and impart it to your employees. It took me more than a year to get any system down on paper. I got so used to working *in* my business, that it took being overwhelmed to push me to start working *on* my business. This change in focus was a turning point for me. And when the time comes when you're ready to have your restaurant work for you, follow this simple advice. Write everything down.

FIRST SIX MONTHS

People like to use yearly benchmarks to depict the health of the business. Particularly, the five-year mark is often seen as the point of your business making it. But I don't think the business itself gets easier over time. The business environment is under constant change and it takes great diligence to be on the pulse of that change and to act on it in a profitable way. However, there is something of incredible value that does get easier over time: your reaction.

I can't predict what your first six months will be like, but I do know that stretch of time will constantly test your strength of character. You will be tugged and pulled in every direction by your customers, employees, family, and even possibly the community at large. Your vision will be questioned and self-doubt will relentlessly try to creep in. There will be incidents that will make you want to give up. Your problems, from one time to another, will seem insurmountable. But if you make it past them enough times and over time, you will discover that what made your challenges big or small was your own reaction to them.

Every problem is an opportunity, an opportunity for you to stretch your mental, emotional and physical capacities. The problems that weighed so heavily on me in the beginning are today laughable. I have thought of giving up when employees called out sick or did not show up for work. I questioned my abilities and future in this industry whenever a complaint was made. My heart was broken when a favorite employee was caught stealing. I didn't realize it at the time, but I was playing victim. And if I had stayed on that mental track, I would have played victim to the demise of my own business.

The first six months of opening your business will feel like the longest stretch of time in your life. There is a lot at stake during this period, and emotions are running high. But take it one day at a time, or even one hour at a time. Over time, business will get easier, and not because of the environment; but because of your confidence in yourself to see it through.

GROWING WITH THE BUSINESS

A t every level and in any industry, a business never has it completely together. Being ready is not a finite point or level of accomplishment, but a *state of being ready to respond.* Just when you think you know all there is to know, things new and unfamiliar will come your way. The manner of your response will determine the outcome. Learning as you go and growing the business over time is honorable and natural. A business is meant to evolve.

Hours before I opened LITM, our cash register was bought from Staples, the toilet was being bolted to the bare concrete floor in the bathroom, and the liquor bottles on the back bar were propped up with scraps of 2-by-4 plywood. It took me almost two years to purchase point-of-sales computers and to renovate our bathroom. My first head bartender taught me how to make drinks. And to this day, I don't know all there is to know about liquor, beer, or wine. I was fully aware that my business setup was incomplete and that I lacked certain knowledge. But I also trusted that I would work at making every day better than the one before. And that included saving up for the equipment I would need to run the restaurant more efficiently, and seeking help from people who had answers to my questions.

Give yourself permission to not know it all. But also commit to responding quickly to the things that need your attention. While markets will vary in tolerance, people tend to be forgiving of a business that they know is growing and finding its way. The key is to communicate with and manage the expectations of your guests. Identify the problem, convey the impact, and work at fixing it. The more intense it is and the more directly it affects your guests, the faster your response must be. Making mistakes is inevitable and even important for a business to get better. Neglect and complacency, however, have no deserving place in business or in life.

MAKE YOUR MOVE

No matter what stage you are with your restaurant, it has been my goal to make you better informed and equipped than you were before reading this book. The information that I have shared with you has come from years of study and practice. I speak from trial and error, from self-exploration and experience. But however much a teacher prepares a student, the lessons and rewards can only come from doing the actual work. What you learn and how you learn them will look different from my experience. But the process will require much of the same from you as it did from me.

Trust in yourself, believe in your work, and have the courage to see it through.

HERE TO HELP

My restaurant was not a one-person effort. And neither is yours. You will need help and you may need it now. I am available through our online community at www.restaurantfromscratch. com. Send me your questions or share what is on your mind. I am here to help.

How can you use this book?

MOTIVATE

EDUCATE

THANK

INSPIRE

PROMOTE

CONNECT

Why have a custom version of *Restaurant from Scratch*?

- Build personal bonds with customers, prospects, employees, donors, and key constituencies
- Develop a long-lasting reminder of your event, milestone, or celebration
- Provide a keepsake that inspires change in behavior and change in lives
- Deliver the ultimate "thank you" gift that remains on coffee tables and bookshelves
- Generate the "wow" factor

Books are thoughtful gifts that provide a genuine sentiment that other promotional items cannot express. They promote employee discussions and interaction, reinforce an event's meaning or location, and they make a lasting impression. Use your book to say "Thank You" and show people that you care.

Restaurant from Scratch is available in bulk quantities and in customized versions at special discounts for corporate, institutional, and educational purposes. To learn more please contact our Special Sales team at:

843.300.4980 • sales@advantageww.com • wwwAdvantageSpecialSales.com

www.ingramcontent.com/pod-product-compliance
Lightning Source LLC
Chambersburg PA
CBHW051525170526
45165CB00002B/608